Borderline
INDIANA

People and Places on State's Borders

By
WENDELL TROGDON

Backroads Press

Distributed by Wendell Trogdon
and Backroads Press
P.O. Box 651
Mooresville, IN 46158

ISBN 0-9642371-3-X

Cover by Gary Varvel
Photos by Fabian Trogdon

Printed by Country Pines Printing
Shoals, Indiana

CONTENTS

Preface . . . . Page 7

The Southeast

Knox County . . . . Page 15
Gibson County . . . . Page 22
Posey County . . . . Page 26
Vanderburgh County . . . . Page 37

Along The Ohio

Warrick County . . . . Page 45
Spencer County . . . . Page 48
Perry County . . . . Page 52
Crawford County . . . . Page 64
Harrison County . . . . Page 69
Floyd County . . . . Page 74
Clark County . . . . Page 76
Jefferson County . . . . Page 81
Switzerland County . . . . Page 86
Ohio County . . . . Page 91
Dearborn County . . . . Page 94

On The East

Franklin County . . . . Page 101
Union County . . . . Page 107

Wayne County. . . . . Page 110

Randolph County . . . . Page 115

Jay County. . . . . Page 122

Adams County . . . . Page 126

Allen County. . . . . Page 132

The Northeast

DeKalb County . . . . Page 135

Steuben County . . . . Page 137

Lagrange County . . . . Page 145

To The North

Elkhart County. . . . . Page 155

St. Joseph County . . . . Page 157

LaPorte County . . . . Page 159

The Northwest

Porter County. . . . . Page 165

Lake County. . . . . Page 168

On The West

Newton County. . . . . Page 179

Benton County . . . . Page 184

Warren County . . . . Page 188

Vermillion County . . . . Page 193

Vigo County . . . . Page 202

Sullivan County . . . . Page 207

DEDICATION

To Charlie Braselton, August Muller, Jim and Jerry Boerner, Mayor Bill Goffinet, Wanda Winchell, Bob Mann, "Bill" Adams, Len and Carol Woelfle, Lois Mora, Bob Hoffman, Larry and Darrell Hofer, Dan Rinkel, Venus and Jim Lukes, Marianne Hutson, Louie Secondino, Robert Axe and all the other helpful and delightful people we met on *Borderline Indiana.*

ACKNOWLEDGMENTS

We are grateful for the assistance of tourism bureaus who provided information about the 36 counties on Indiana's border. We also referred often to the book *Indiana: A New Historical Guide* and to the *Indiana Recreation Guide* published by the division of state parks. Much of our trip was over roads found in the atlas, *Indiana County Maps*, a unit of Thomas Publications.

PREFACE

Cypress trees, believed to form the northern-most grove in the nation, thrive in a swamp near the Wabash.

Croaks, deep, resonate, constant, seemingly eternal, rise from a pond, the only sound in a sea of silence. It is spring, mating season and the male frogs are passionate.

Sheldrake ducks, their plumage black and white, swim in the backwaters that remain from the flooded river.

A few miles away a heron flutters onto a tree limb to rest. If there is a paradise for wildlife, it is here in southwestern Indiana.

We are along White River near where it separates Knox and Gibson Counties on roads seldom traveled, on this the first in a month of days we will spend on the border of a state so filled with wonders few can appreciate the treasures it holds. Our mission is to reveal the secrets that remain on Indiana's fringes.

* * *

We have chosen to call this book *Borderline Indiana*, not because borderline is synonymous with ambiguous, cryptic, indecisive, inexplicit or obscure. Indiana is none of these things.

The definitions "mysterious, enigmatic," are more applicable to a state whose borders, straight at times, irregular elsewhere, stretch for more than 1,000 miles.

Indiana is, indeed, a state of contrasts, endless differences in its terrain, its resources, its history and its people. It is its variations, sharply defined, that creates its mystique and adds to its charm.

Its boundaries were drawn by men with surveyor equipment; cut by the Ohio and Wabash Rivers as they meandered down the paths of least resistance, nicked by Lake Michigan on the northwest corner.

The terrain is never dull as it changes from majestic cliff outcroppings on the Ohio, to rolling hills, to endless fields to the sand dunes in the north.

Its soil, too, is varied, sandy along rivers, clay in the south, loam in the central sections, muck in the north. Downstate, fields may be fenced patches in hollows between hills; upstate, seemingly endless acreage that stretches unrestricted toward the horizon.

To the south are river towns older than the state itself, historic places called Vincennes, Troy, Evansville, Lawrenceburg, all named for men and places long forgotten.

To the north, cities are a century younger, their growth faster, with suburbs where homes rise like mushrooms after spring rains.

The atmosphere changes too, from the unpopulated south where clear air is as fresh as new-mown hay to the industrial northwest where whisky-brown smog is laced with the smell of sulphur and oil.

Its people — men and women now grouped as Hoosiers under an ethnic umbrella — come from genealogical backgrounds as different as Gary and Mount Vernon, as diverse as Tell City and Michigan City.

They live in quiet conclaves on the Ohio, towns called Rome and Derby; in urbanized metroplexes, places defined as the Calumet and South Bend/Mishawaka; on farms where houses are miles apart, in new suburbs where yesterday's cornfield is tomorrow's housing addition.

For the most part, they travel the slow lanes in the south where tomorrow is a distant date, today is to enjoy. On the open road, they return waves, stop to help a stranded motorist, are less likely to blast their car horns at errant drivers.

In the industrial north, they travel express routes of life, today a brief stop on the way to next week. Life, it appears, is harder, work more stressful, money more important, survival more difficult.

As individuals, however, all possess some old-fashioned Hoosier traits, hospitality, friendliness, a sense of pride in their state. Most seem reasonably content with their stations in life.

* * *

We resume now this preview of a few of the places and people you will meet on this trip through the 36 counties that help shape *Borderline Indiana*.

* * *

Its arm nodding slowly and continually, a pump brings oil from deep within the ground, then sends it to a storage tank nearby. Oil, like coal, is one of southwestern Indiana's resources.

South in Posey County, ostriches — a new source of agricultural revenue — strut on at least five farms, seemingly proud despite their confinement.

Proud, too, are farmers who tend the fields in the Wabash bottoms around New Harmony. It is the yields from the rich land that has allowed them to pay property taxes to keep the town's high school, with an enrollment of less than 100, from being swallowed into a consolidation.

Not everyone elsewhere, though, cares for high taxes. August Muller has spent his 80-plus years in the toe of Indiana, down near where the Wabash meets the Ohio.

He looks around his farm and asks, "You know what? My dad bought this ground for $10 an acre in 1898. Would you believe that now, we've got the fancy high school and the fancy swimmin' pool (at Mount Vernon) and you know my taxes on this 158 acres is $10 an acre a year. I'm buyin' this farm ever' year. Ain't it a sight?"

Farmers are friendly. Up the Ohio between Mount Vernon and Evansville, brothers Jim and Jerry Boerner stop working on a John Deere tractor to talk.

They look across the road at the brick building. It was the West Franklin school, which opened in 1906, the year their father was born. "That's where we got some of our education, such as it is," Jerry laughs.

On up river is the famed Dogtown Tavern, named because customers once had to walk past dogs left at the door by owners who sought refreshments after hunting the bayous and woods.

Past Evansville and its Riverfront Park and historic downtown is Newburgh, where the new blends with the old. One of the state's oldest towns (founded in 1803), it is home to one of Indiana's newest "characters," Angie Sinclair's Tootie Tittlemouse, which appears in at least four colorfully illustrated children's books.

Up river are the Newburgh Locks and Dam, one in a series of five on the Ohio along Indiana's border which make the Ohio an important artery for the nation's commerce.

Viewing platforms at Newburgh, as at Uniontown downstream and Cannelton and Markland up river, allow visitors to watch as barges are raised and lowered from 342 feet above sea level at

Uniontown near the Ohio-Wabash delta, to 455 feet at Markland, up river from Vevay.

Mayors of river cities are their own spokespersons. At Tell City, Bill Goffinet boasts of his city's "great quality of life." "It's one of the prettiest parts of the state. We have the hills and trees and a tremendous amount of recreational opportunities the river affords," he explains.

Rock outcroppings form a ledge along Ind. 66 squeezing it in places against the river.

At the town of Rome, the post office is the social center of town. Postmaster Wanda Winchell offers a visitor a seat in one of the white vinyl chairs on the porch. "I bought these chairs so people who come here early can wait for their mail or sit and visit with each other after they pick it up."

Up river from Magnet and Buzzard's Roost, Melinda and Ron Koopman have one of the best views along the Ohio's entire 350-mile route along Indiana's base. "That's Meade County, Kentucky," Melinda explains, pointing across the river. "It's the only place in Indiana where you can look north into Kentucky."

At New Albany, Clarksville and Jeffersonville, residents are proud to be Hoosiers. "The Sunny Side of Louisville," they call their towns, each with its own history, its own role in the growth of Indiana.

At Madison, smoke rises from the giant smokestacks at a generating station, one of many along the river which is a source of power as well as for transportation and recreation. High above the river is Clifty Falls, one of the jewels in Indiana's State Park system.

Upstream at Brooksburg, Charles "Bill" Adams watches the tiny store for his mother. "She's 88 and she ought to be out of here, but I can't get her to leave. She can't watch it and I don't wanta. I retired once," he laughs.

Len and Carol Woelfle moved to Switzerland County from Cincinnati. Carol says, "It's different down here, completely. You know all your neighbors here, even if they are ten miles away. In Cincinnati, you sometimes didn't know who lived across the street."

North of the Ohio where it ends its zigzag path along Indiana's south boundary, the steep hills are being filled with expensive homes. Buckeyes are becoming Hoosiers, finding land cheaper, life less hectic than in nearby Cincinnati.

Bob Hoffman and his wife run a country store at Mount Carmel, a Franklin County town. It isn't easy for a small business-man to operate in an era of Wal-Marts. "We try to keep a lot of things. It's not a hugely-successful business, but it makes a little money. We have a school bus route and I write health and life insurance," he explains.

Two border towns along the Ohio line prove Hoosiers and Buckeyes can co-exist. At College Corner, the grade school strad-dles the state line, "Indiana" above the west door, "Ohio" over the east door. All the students move on to Union County High School at Liberty in Indiana. To the north, two Union Cities share the border.

Some towns seem lost in time, ghosts of the past. At Salamo-nia in Jay County, a gravity-flow gasoline pump remains in front of an abandoned general store. The post office is out of business, mail left in boxes out front for residents.

Almost every Indiana town has something to promote. Near the start of the Wabash River just east of the Ohio line, visitors entering a community along marsh land are informed: "New Cory-don, 1821. Home of the Blue Heron."

In Adams County, Amish buggies almost outnumber cars along some roads. Some drivers pull to the side of the road, a courtesy to vehicles behind them.

At Pleasant Mills, Eldana Edgell wonders how long the town can keep its post office. She has been in charge for three years as "a postmaster relief," yet uncertain whether she'll ever be postmaster. A community loses its identity when its schools are closed and its postmark is lost.

Some towns have no restaurants. Some, like Butler in DeKalb County, are more fortunate. "Mom's Eaten Haus" serves good food and gives customers a view of the past. Its walls are lined with mementos and pictures, a reminder of a time that now exists only in antiques and memories.

Lakes, many created by the great glaciers, dot northeastern Indiana, making the area a recreation center for Hoosiers and visitors from Michigan and Ohio. Bait shops are big business in the area.

Hoosiers are entrepreneurs, imaginative, creative. Harold L. Nelson is "Hubcap Harold," willing to "buy, sell or trade," at his barn on Ind. 120 in Steuben County.

Communities need spots to relax, swap stories, quench thirst. Hap's Tap, a restaurant bar on Ind. 20 just west of I-69, is busy at 8 a.m., serving breakfast to customers interested in the weather, home mortgages and sports results.

Across northern Indiana, residents are a bit more reserved than downstate, less likely to volunteer information, to give their life stories as are Hoosiers to the south.

Dan Rinkel is not one of them. He is at work — just like three generations of Rinkels before him — at 160-year-old Greenfield Mills on Fawn River. It is here the Rinkel family grinds flour from various grains for an assortment of uses and provides power for a dozen or so homes from its hydro-generating station.

Rinkel offers a friendly greeting, volunteers information for the mill is living history worth sharing with outsiders.

There is no fear of strangers in rural areas. A Mennonite woman pauses on her bicycle in a light shower and reveals we have found the town of Seyberts. "This is it," she says, "it" being two or three farm homes.

New suburban communities line sections of the Indiana Toll Road, close enough to jobs in Mishawaka and South Bend, far enough away to avoid the congestion of the cities.

Some county roads offer hidden gems. On a ten-mile section of LaPorte County Road 1000 North are: The Hesston Bar, one of the area's favorite dining spots; a one room school built in 1890 now used as a parsonage, a church with furnishings dating back to 1867, a cemetery with a panoramic view of the country side, the Hesston Steam Museum and Christmas tree, fruit tree, blueberry and horse farms.

Not far from Michigan City is the first section of the Indiana Dunes National Lakeshore. It is here visitors can scale 123-feet high Mt. Baldy, called "the tallest living sand dune on the southern shore of Lake Michigan."

Lake Michigan is lined with beeches, homes from elegant to modest, expensive communities, gray overcast cities, steel mills by the mile, oil refineries, marinas and sand dunes.

The sky is overcast, penetrated only by a bright sun. The smell of molten steel, the odor of sulphur, penetrate the nostrils.

South of the congestion in lower Lake County, Reichert's Tavern is open, thriving as Brunswick's only commercial enterprise and offering beer, wine, sandwiches . . . and endless conversation. Brunswick, like other towns near metropolitan areas, is changing, a new housing development bringing a new way of life to an old town.

Further south, however, another old town remains untouched by new development. Sumava Resorts was born in another time, in another era, back in the late 1920s when developers from Chicago bought land along the Kankakee and brought would-be buyers on passenger trains to hear their sales spiels.

The vast prairie begins just south of Sumava Resorts in Newton County, allowing Kentland to claim it is the town "where agriculture and industry meet."

It is in this area where fields stretch across the horizon, broken only by property lines, drainage ditches and county roads. It is here that the trend toward bigger farms, fewer farmers, is obvious. Elevators, tall beacons higher than church spires, and storage granaries are as expansive on some farms as they once were along railroads in small towns.

On Ind. 71 down the western boundary, farm tractors outnumber cars. A pheasant shuffles across the pavement into a corn field, safe from cars . . . and hunters until fall.

In Ambia, a resident agrees the town, like hundreds of others, started its downward slide when it lost its school. Only a memorial on the school ground remains at what once was the artery that gave the community a heartbeat and a sense of purpose. People remain, but retail businesses, stores, restaurants are gone. A cup of coffee for a motorist is six miles or so away in another town.

State Line City south in Warren County has changed, too. "Not much left here," says Milton Anderson, looking west across town to where Indiana and Illinois meet and State Line City becomes Illiana.

The beer is cheap, the talk cheaper at Lance's Hut in Blanford, an old coal mining town north of Terre Haute. Marianne Hutson, at work behind the bar, talks about Blanford's past. "There were so many taverns there was no room for churches." Only her place remains . . . and there now is space in town for churches.

Down the road is Universal, another coal mining community where Louie Secondino, 98, has lived since 1912. He ran a grocery in town from 1914 to 1949, saw the town rise and fall, noted that change is as inevitable as the seasons.

South of Terre Haute, Robert Axe puts down his welder and talks, easy, openly, interestingly. He is building a horse drawn plow in a time of giant farm tractors. Axe grew up in Terre Haute, where he learned to appreciate the horses he fed for a deliveryman. Axe still farms 20 acres with horses. "You don't have to get off a tractor to open gates when you farm with horses," he grins.

This is a brief preview of some of the places and people on the borders of Indiana.

Join us now for a more leisurely odyssey along *Borderline Indiana.*

The Southeast

KNOX COUNTY

Indiana's first county, formed in 1790. Population 40,000. Named for Henry Knox, a Revolutionary War general and an adviser to George Washington. Rich agriculture county, noted for its peaches and melons.

VINCENNES

Nee: Fort Sackville

It seems appropriate to begin a tour of Indiana's borders at Vincennes, its cradle. It is Indiana's oldest city, its first settlement dating back to 1732.

Vincennes' history is subject for novels. Its landmarks mark the city's significance in the development of a nation. Vincennes is not for a quick visit. There is too much to see, too much of the past to record.

It was here the French established an outpost and fur trading center, which later was occupied by the British. It was here where young Lt. Col. George Rogers Clark and his men took Fort Sackville from the British, who later regained control. It was to Vincennes — over 180 miles of flooded lowlands — that Clark and his troops returned from Kaskaskie. They surprised the British and retook the fort for the United States February 23, 1779.

The George Rogers Clark National Historic Park is on the banks of the Wabash River in Vincennes, which was the capital of the Indiana Territory.

A replica of the Western Sun print shop remains near the site of the territorial capitol. The newspaper, started in 1804 as the *Indiana Gazette*, later became the *Western Sun* and in a merger in 1931 became the *Vincennes Sun-Commercial*, which still serves the area.

It was here James Maurice Thompson wrote the ever-popular *"Alice of Old Vincennes"* and it was here where comedian Red Skelton grew up. It was here where Vincennes University was started in 1801 as Jefferson Academy.

And it is here Indiana's role in the birth of a nation can be relived.

* * *

It is spring, a pleasant sunny week with day-time temperatures in the 70s. We have started our trip south along the Wabash, a river the Indians called "Wah-bah-shik-ki" and which the French corrupted to "Qubache" or "Quabache." One interpretation of Wah-bah-shik-ki is "pure white," another "water over white stones."

ST. THOMAS

Past And Present

Like dozens of hamlets, St. Thomas is a church community, built around the Apostle Roman Catholic Church, which has served the area for more than 150 years.

Its past is buried in the nearby cemetery. Its present is centered around the church and the shelter house, the hub of social activity as well as religious worship for the German and French community.

St. Thomas is in the Wabash Valley, not far from the river, and water is plentiful. A new irrigation system, mounted on rubber tires and stretching for a quarter of a mile, is being assembled in a field. A well, 36 inches in diameter being drilled just off the road, will provide a constant source of water when dry weather arrives.

Oil wells are in operation nearer the river which sometimes floods the bottom land despite the levee on its banks, a half-mile away. High water is always a threat, was even back in the days when Indiana was young and George Rogers Clark traveled the bottoms.

CLARK'S ADVANCE

"No Dry Ground"

An access to the Wabash in Knox County

An historical marker at a place marked "Clark's Advance" cryptically recalls that day back in 1779 when Clark prepared to retake Fort Sackville.

"We stopped on the second hill of the same Mamelle, there being no dry ground near us on one side for many leagues. Our pilots say we cannot get along. That is impossible, the whole Army being over. We encamped. Rain all this day. No provisions. Feb. 22. Col. Clark encourages his men, which gave them spirits to march on in the water. Those that were weak and faintish from so much fatigue went in the canoes."

(It is assumed a mamelle is an elevation of land).

The message was from the journal of a Major Bowman. An arrow below the marker points to the mamelle.

We reach Clark's Advance over a concrete road, the kind counties built in the early days of the auto. At river's edge we find the Clark's Landing public access operated by the Department of Natural Resources "in cooperation with Burt Alexander."

There is no indication who Burt Alexander is and there is no one to ask. We learn later he donated the land to provide entry to the river.

Across the river is the Illinois town of St. Francisville, which is build on a rise away from water's edge.

BEAL

Mary and John

To the south on Knox County Road 900 West is Beal, a community near the river, with bottom land stretching for miles on the Indiana side.

The cemetery, old and dotted with nine cedar trees, gives some indications of the community's long history. Twin wooden crosses painted red, about three feet high, are marked with the names of Mary and John Strange. Neither is marked with dates of birth or death.

It is March, but already people are at work in their gardens, happy the winter appears to have ended early.

At the Pentecostal Church, the message board reads, "Baptism in Jesus' name infilling of the Holy Ghost." It is the first of a score of church doctrines we will record on our travels.

Beal is an undefined area with a dozen frame houses and manufactured homes along a single road. One of the homes is large, well maintained with its own tennis court.

DOWN ON THE LEVEE

Delicate Balance

We encounter the first of miles of crushed stone roads we will encounter. Traffic in many areas will be too light to justify the expense of pavement.

David Sheren is on duty at a pumping station operated as part of the Brevoort Levee in cooperation with the Army Corps of Engineers. Giant pumps are at work inside the brick building next to the levee along the Wabash.

It is a delicate balance, this effort to maintain peace between the land and the river. Sheren, who says he works for Mack Montgomery, the levee commissioner, explains how the station operates:

"When the river starts falling and the water equals out, that's when they shut the pumps off. When the river gets below the ditch stage, then the gates are open so the water can run from drainage ditches into the river."

He's on duty for 24 hours at a time, but his work place is reasonably comfortable, a cot for rest, a TV for relaxation.

* * *

We zigzag on rural roads over asphalt, gravel and chuckholes to County Road 1100 West through bottom land protected by the levees.

ORRVILLE

Passed By Time

The Wabash makes one of its incursions west in southern Knox County. On a paved road toward the river, we pass a brick building. "School No. 4, Orrville," an engraving in stone reads. Large trees have grown up around the outside walls.

On an isolated dusty road nearer the river, a woman walks her dog. "That is all that is left of Orrville," she says, looking toward the school that once was the center of a community.

We are miles from any store. A few homes have satellite dishes. Utility poles carry two lines, one for electricity, one for telephones, none for cable television.

Two John Deere tractors are lined up at road's edge, like race cars, ready to get the jump on spring once the flag drops on another planting season.

DECKER CHAPEL
Sense of Purpose

There are no stores in Decker Chapel. There is no school, has been none since a consolidation sent high school students to South Knox High.

The site of the school, which had operated since 1912, is marked by a stone marker. Nearby is the Decker Township Community Center, a metal building which has given the area a sense of purpose since 1976.

Rev. Sue Gauck is minister of the Decker Chapel United Methodist Church. Evelyn Owens is the lay minister. The role of women in today's ministries is growing, we will learn on this excursion around Indiana.

RIVER'S EDGE
Cypress and Swamps

We pass a swampy area where the mating call of frogs is continuous, drowning out the pings of pebbles propelled against the wheel wells of our pickup.

A young man, his beard reddish like his long hair, is walking along the road. "Name's Derick Field," he says. "We live at Vincennes but farm down here. Things aren't going well this morning. My planter broke," he explains quickly.

He rides in the back of the truck to the nearest house where he can call for help. He suggests, "You should drive back toward the river and find Cypress Swamp. That's the farthest north, cypress trees grow. Some of them are as big as your S-10 Chevy and they are worth seeing."

He thanks us. We thank him, then follow his directions, past bottomland grain farms where some cattle graze, but few hogs are raised. A duck crossing sign is posted on Knox County Road 1800 South.

Cypress trees grow in swamp near Wabash

To reach Cypress Swamp, we again drive past the Orrville School, continue toward the river, then turn south to a point where trees line each side of the crushed stone road.

The swamp is on each side of the road. There are indeed cypress trees in the green pond, some huge, the trunk of one, as Derick said, would more than fill the bed of the pickup. Cypress knees protrude from the water. It's a scene that seems out of place in a northern state.

Frogs croak in the swamp, constant, like locusts on their 17-year visits. If it is mating season, the frogs are eager to engage in procreation.

Some fields are still flooded and we see what appear to be sheldrake ducks with black and white plumage in the ponded water just south of the swamp.

A heron flutters down and parks on a tree limb. A number of oil wells pump continuously, silently. This is an area where oil, water and wildlife live in harmony.

We return east toward U.S. 41 along White River. The roads are rough, some of the crushed stones as big as volleyballs. The terrain is more rolling, the fields smaller away from the Wabash bottoms.

GIBSON COUNTY

Southwestern Indiana, set off as a county from Knox County in 1813. Population 32,000. Named for Brig. Gen. John Gibson, an Indian fighter who also was secretary of the Indiana territory. Noted for its watermelons, cantaloupes, coal and oil.

THE CONFLUENCE
Two Rivers Into One

Gibson County Road 350 North leads west of Patoka on U.S. 41 past oil wells.

Soft drink cans in a net sack have been tossed into a drainage ditch, another example of man's disrespect for his environment. A muffler is in the road, having lost its battle to stay on a car on the washboard-like road.

Just west of the Wabash, which separates Indiana and Illinois, a community stretches along the south bank of White River. Most of

the homes are elevated six to eight feet off the ground as a protection against flooding. Even a mini barn is on stilts. These are
vacation get-aways, campers and mobile homes with names like
"Shady Shack" and "Summer Place."

Confluence of Wabash and White Rivers

We are in search of the confluence of White and Wabash. We
ask two men at work on a four-wheeler if we can drive to the point
where the rivers meet.

"Not in that," one says, looking at the pickup. "I could in this,"
he says turning to the vehicle he has been repairing.

He tells us to cross the Ind. 64 bridge to Mt. Carmel, Illinois,
then take Fifth Street back east to the river where the convergence
of the rivers can be seen from a park.

His directions are easy to follow. Several other motorists have
parked to watch the rivers blend into one, a harmony of water,
peaceful even when both streams are high.

ALONG THE WABASH
"A Mile For a Camel"

We drive south from Ind. 64 on the Indiana side of the Wabash past PSI Energy's Gibson Generating Station, which has a park on the river for its employees.

Blacktop pavement ends, roads again are gravel and stone. The land is flat, the only elevation the levee. We turn east on Gibson County Road 800 West, which has three feet high concrete bridge abutments on the sides of narrow bridges. Fluorescent paint warns motorists of the hazards.

We are in search of the community of Shelton when we meet Charlie Braselton.

Men and women like Braselton offset any displeasure from rough roads. He's a genuine Hoosier, friendly, open, eager to talk. He recalls the Shelton of his youth:

"When I started farming right after the war, I used to smoke. I quit. I got smart," he interjects. "I farmed a field about a mile-and-half from Shelton. When I ran out of cigarettes, I'd have to walk to Shelton to get a pack. You've heard them say, 'I'd walk a mile for a camel?' Well, I was that dumb. At that time, there was a store there and two or three houses. Now, everything is gone except for the man who farms the ground."

He also talks about Crawleyville, which also is on the old map we show him:

"I was down there just the other day. Someone is living in one of the few places that are left, but you wouldn't walk in because it is so trashy around there. That town used to have a store and a church, but that was years ago."

Braselton farmed and carried a rural mail route before retiring to his rural home. "I worked my tail off. Drove 84 miles a day on the mail route then farmed when I got home. I worked so late (driving a farm tractor) I couldn't sit anymore. But I managed."

We drive to Owensville, then west in order to remain near the river. Past the town of Johnson, giant metal granaries dot the farm land which is visible for miles up and down the Wabash lowlands. Houses are few, far between.

Near the Wabash the land isn't as rich or open. Bridges over drainage ditches are protected by wooden rails. Some have iron sides that rise six or eight feet.

Charlie Braselton was correct. Crawleyville is an unsightly place, two houses surrounded by junk, including a clothes dryer.

We follow the Wabash south as closely as roads permit. Some land is marked "Private Property," others "No Trespassing." It appears that in this area the shabbier the property, the more likely it will be posted with an off limits sign.

A pump is operating near an abandoned house that has collapsed, giving some indication that an oil well may not necessarily make a land owner wealthy. Oil storage tanks are near the river.

Covered bridge in southwestern Gibson County

The only remaining covered bridge in Gibson County is in its far southwestern corner near the intersection of Road 1600 West and 650 South. It no longer is in use, but it is well-painted with a good roof. A Farm Bureau sign offers a $1,000 reward for information about anyone who might damage it.

Graffiti, some in good taste, some not, is evidence spray can artists have visited the bridge more for mischief than for its history. Initials remain carved in time on the timbers.

South of the bridge a homeowner cleans around an oil pump. The land is low, likely to flood and some oil storage tanks are elevated off the ground.

Gibson County ends at a sharp point against the Wabash at the site of Webb's Ferry, which no longer operates.

POSEY COUNTY

Southwestern-most point in Indiana, shaped by the Wabash on the west, the Ohio on the south. Population 27,000. Formed in 1814. Named for Maj. Gen. Thomas Posey, a Revolutionary War general and governor of the Indiana Territory. Farm land is rich, but the county has become industrialized since the opening of the Southwind Maritime Center on the Ohio.

GRIFFIN
No More "Tornadoes"

We cross from Gibson into Posey County and head south past an oil storage center operated by Equinox Oil Company. Except for that we seem to be almost out of civilization, at least temporarily.

A blacktop road leads to the town of Griffin just off Interstate 64.

The Griffin High School gym, once the home of the Griffin Tornadoes, still stands, but students now attend North Posey High.

This is a residential town, one that appears to take pride in itself. There are churches, antique shops, a senior citizen's center. Griffin, it appears, is a quiet place to raise a family or retire. A street-side sign offers, "Puppies to go."

We take a county road south which crosses the Black River on a steel bridge manufactured by the Toledo Bridge Company in 1892. Nice houses and vast fields line the river's edge. An old channel of the Wabash allows Illinois a peninsula into what would have been part of Indiana in this area.

NEW HARMONY
Past and Present

Further south, Wabash bottom fields grow larger. It is income from some of these farms that allow farmers to pay taxes so New Harmony can keep its high school, defying consolidation. The school has less than 100 students, making it one of the three smallest public high schools in the state.

Farmers and retirees are drinking coffee and trading stories at the Main Street Cafe at 6 a.m., an hour too early for tourists. Amid the good-natured taunting, one of the men offers to plow another's garden; two others plan to swap work. In small towns, residents know each other, offer assistance when help is needed.

New Harmony is an ideal spot for a quiet overnight or weekend visit, especially for students of history. It was here that George Rapp came in the early 1800s to establish the Harmony Society and plan a cooperative community for Christian communal living. Called Harmonie by Rapp, the community covered almost 1,500 acres and included 175 or so homes.

Robert Owen bought the settlement in 1825 when the Rappites returned to Pennsylvania. Many of the buildings erected by the Harmonists can be seen on a walking tour of the town.

Rooms are usually available at the lodge-like New Harmony Inn where dining at either the Red Geranium Restaurant or the Bayou Grill is recommended.

South of town off Ind. 69, the landscape is unsullied as it extends over ravines to the Wabash. Cabins and camp sites may be reserved for overnight or weekly visits at Harmonie State Park, called "a trail lover's paradise."

SAVAH
Time and Temperature

Two pumps bring oil from wells on the Posey County 4-H fairgrounds on Ind. 69. Black sheep graze on a hill along the highway. Ostriches walk proudly on a farm in the area.

We turn west toward the river to a spot on the map called Savah. The road, rough and dusty, rises and falls with the terrain. A barn has collapsed, the victim of age. Wheels from antique dump rakes now "decorate" the entrance to a farm.

A "Welcome to Savah" sign on the side of a concrete block building greets visitors. The store no longer is in business but a thermometer remains tacked to its front door.

The four-room brick Walker District 1 School, its bell in place in its tower, is now the Savah Community Center. The pump where students once quenched their thirst remains out front. A basketball goal on the grounds has had little use for there are few youngsters in the area.

A sign in the community asks, "Are You Prayed Up?" It's a question each passerby will need to answer for himself or herself.

WELBORN and GRAFTON
And Upton, Too

Soil does not appear to be too rich in this area, but oil is a resource of revenue nearer the Wabash.

Less than two miles from Savah, we find what remains of the community of Welborn, a mere ghost of its past. When its place on the Seaboard System no longer was an asset, it died like hundreds of other railroad towns. Call Welborn a tombstone in the cemetery of life.

A half-mile to the northwest, the railroad crosses the swamp land, spans the Wabash and enters Illinois.

This area along the river may be remote, but it is not out of touch. Satellite dishes are common, swimming pools are seen in some lawns. One farm has an airplane ready to taxi toward a journey from its runway. American flags are numerous. Some fly over state flags at well kept homes, others from run down houses. Patriotism is a common denominator, uniting the poor and the affluent.

South of Savah and Welborn is a three-way intersection identified on the map as Grafton, a community with a new bridge over Indian Creek, a prosperous farm operation, an unfenced junk yard, one house and an unoccupied house trailer.

Two paved roads lead into the hamlet of Upton, which also is on the Seaboard System Railroad. One of 20 or so homes has a "Sold" sign out front, an indication that some people prefer the solitude of small communities that have no post offices, no convenience stores, no retail outlets.

DEEP POCKETS

Tombstone Territory

Ancient three-tombstone cemetery in Posey County

We drive south into the deepest pocket of Indiana, down into the peninsula formed by the twisting Wabash and the meandering Ohio.

Fields extend for miles, as far as the eyes can see, toward the river, offering a look at a productive agricultural area of which few people are familiar.

On the road south three tombstones rise from a cemetery that is elevated three feet above the cornfield that surrounds it. It is the burial place for pioneers C. S. Jeffries, born January 12, 1825, died in 1852, his wife and their daughter. Time has all but erased names and dates from the markers on this tiny plot 50 by 100 feet.

Trees that had grown 8-10 inches in diameter have been cut, vegetation cleared from the graves, perhaps for the first time in decades. It is obvious someone has taken time to improve the tiny cemetery, perhaps as a tribute to pioneers who opened the area for people who followed.

Nearer the river, some farm houses are built on elevations to avoid being damaged when the low land around them floods. The landscape is dominated by grain elevators, storage bins, large fields and irrigation equipment. Some roads are paved, some coated with river gravel. None are marked by name or number.

We are in Point Township, which is an appropriate name for it is near the junction of the two rivers.

AUGUST MULLER
Man of the Land

Not far from the church, a man works in a grove of trees 300 yards off the road, his pickup nearby.

"August Muller," he introduces himself. He greets us on the bright warm morning as a friend, not as a stranger, weaving us into his search for scrap iron and collectibles as easily as he roots out an item of value.

He is a big man, his face leathered by farm work, his mind sharpened by an endless curiosity. August has cleared the underbrush among the trees that covered what had once been a heap of discarded items from his house, barn and tool shed. "Scrap iron is pretty high right now," he explains, referring to its price.

"Find any antiques?" we inquire.

"Oh yeah. Know what this is?" he asks and smiles when we identify it correctly as an item used to lift lids off old-time kitchen ranges so more wood could be added.

He looks pleased to be talking to someone who remembers the past. "If a fellow polished that thing up, it might bring a whole lot at an antique market. I ought to take some of these things up there and sell them."

Up there is Mount Vernon, the county seat up river on the Ohio.

"Bet you can't guess what that is," he says, fingering what looks like a piece of copper. "You ain't old enough to know that stuff," he teases. He identifies the copper as "an impeller off a water pump."

August finds what he says is a diaphragm from the horn on an old phonograph. It reminds him of a story.

"We always thought that song . . .," he pauses to think. "Goldarn it, I sung it last night," he says, then remembers it is called, "Don't be Angry With Me, Darling?" "We thought that was a new song. But a 1906 Sears Roebuck catalog I found had a list of 50 songs and that was one of them."

He keeps talking and searching for items. "I was born right over there in that house. I had eight brothers and a sister and I'm the only one who farmed."

"Copper," he says, flipping another item onto a pile.

"I retired from farming in '82. My son does the work now. I've got 158 acres, but he (his son) farms more than that.

"You know what?" he asks, then answers himself. "My dad bought this ground for $10 an acre in 1898. Would you believe that now we've got the fancy high school and the fancy swimmin' pool (at Mount Vernon) and you know my taxes on this 158 acres are $10 an acre a year. I'm buyin' this farm ever' year. Ain't it a sight? And taxes keep going up and up."

We let August talk uninterrupted. He is an excellent source of information. "When dad arrived in this area and stopped over there (pointing to the house), he had to cut a tree to have room to park the wagon. That was in 1898. That was before any of the land was cleared.

"This part of the country once had a house on every 40 acres. Used to be a post office down there at what they called Roach's Landing. And there was a saloon, too. Stage coaches went through there so often they made a cut in the hill. We used to have a store right down there by the church. Now we have to go to Mount Vernon to buy a loaf of bread." (Mount Vernon is eight miles to the northeast.)

He talks about floods. "The water was 35 miles wide here in 1937 and no one drowned. The rivers (Wabash and Ohio) meet right down there," he explains, pointing to the southwest.

August is a man who says what he thinks. "The DNR (Department of Natural Resources) wants to buy up all this ground for a home for wolves and coyotes and deer. You know what that means. DNR don't pay no taxes. So that means those who stay will have to make up the loss (in tax revenue). It's not fair. Some of them sportsmen out of Indianapolis come down here and they want the deer and birds so thick they don't have to look for them. If sportsmen want this land to be layin' out they ought to pay taxes on it.

"The DNR would buy my land if I'd sell it. They're after my neighbor to sell." Miller, however, is staying put. This is home and his sweat and tears are deep in the rich bottom land.

"I cleared all of this," he explains, waving his arms over part of the farm. "We grubbed the stumps and when the trees were out of the holes we cut them off and sold the trees for logs. We worked 33 days the winter of 1961, clearin' this field."

He apologizes for not hearing a question. "I wore out so many tractors I can't hear. I got a bad ear. I like to play music with them guys up at Evansville, but it gets so noisy I can't understand what they're adoin. I just foller them. I play the guitar. It's billed as bluegrass, but it's mostly country.

"I have three or four guitars and two banjos and a fiddle, but I don't have no one to play music with down here. And my arthritis is so bad at times I have to quit playing."

He mentions his German heritage, says he has two brothers who spell their last name Mueller, instead of Muller and says his grandfather fought in the Civil War at Vicksburg.

"Now they come along with this Afro-American bull. Why don't we say we're German American?" he asks.

He doesn't wait for a response. He digs out another piece of metal from the dirt. "Ain't that cast iron?"

He knows it is. He's being polite to a stranger. We start to leave. "Lookie here," he says, holding up another item for the antique shop.

It's difficult to leave a man with a reservoir of knowledge almost as old as the century.

ROACH'S LANDING

A Family Remembered

A trailer across from the Point Township Nazarene Church is a recycling center of sorts for the area, containing thousands of discarded soft drink cans.

"Welcome" says a sign at the big brick church. It is open, but no one is there on this Tuesday morning.

At a fork in the road near the river, a marker notes: "The Hughes Farm, 1898-1974. Pearl Yeida and Ed Hughes, loving parents of Kelly, Stoy and Media." Signs indicate the farm is at the junction of Roach's Landing Road and Bone Bank Road.

The asphalt ends, but Bone Bank Road continues to an inlet on the Wabash called "Oak Grove." It is a fenced river resort marked "Private Property," an isolated resort as far from the center of the state anyone can go and still be in Indiana.

We pass another nature preserve further south where more cypress trees grow in the swamp land. Not far away, visitors are warned at Mobile Oil Company's Maggie Murphy lease that hydrogen sulphine gas may be present.

We are as close as we can get to the confluence of the Wabash and Ohio, the southernmost tip of Indiana. It is there that the storied Wabash ends its 475-mile journey.

Few Hoosiers realize that this part of Indiana is 30 miles further south than Louisville, Ky.

UNIONTOWN LOCKS

Controlling the Ohio

On the paved entrance to the Uniontown Locks and Dam a heron stands in a pool of water, then leaves as a car approaches. Herons, it appears, are numerous in southwestern Indiana.

The locks are across the Ohio from the small Kentucky community of Uniontown. It is here on the Indiana side that visitors can view barges and boats as they are raised and lowered through the locks. It is the first of a series of five locks and dams on this trip up the Ohio in Indiana.

The system of locks and dams — at Uniontown as well as at Newburgh, Cannelton, Louisville and Markland — raise and lower boats and barges a total of 113 feet (from 342 feet above sea level at Uniontown to 455 feet at Markland) as they pass Indiana's border.

It is the locks that have made the Ohio an important artery for commerce and industry in the nation's heartland. In the last two decades, Indiana has opened river ports at Mount Vernon and Jeffersonville, which import and export tons of cargo over the nation's inland waterway system.

HOVEY LAKE
It's for the Birds

We remain near the Ohio as it curves to the north. Small fields extend to the tree-lined river. The road, covered by water in spots, turns almost to mud as it severs a corn field. The few cabins along the river are weekend summer retreats and there is no traffic on a week day.

The road is paved as we enter the Hovey Lake state fish and wildlife area, a 4,400-acre lowland area noted for its fishing and hunting and cypress swamps.

We spot only one fisherman on the water.

"We'll get busy in another month when the crappie fishing is good, then again in the fall when duck hunting season opens," says Brad Feaster, one of the DNR employees.

Robin Tron, another employee, adds, "Hunters come from everywhere. Fishermen are usually local people or from Evansville."

Mrs. Tron knows the area, says it is called "Huvey" not "Hoevey." She remembers when the town of Hovey to the north had a blacksmith shop, an Oddfellows Hall and a general store from which a huckster wagon traveled the rural areas. The road (Ind. 69) was relocated away from the town, which withered without traffic. Only its name on maps is a reminder of its past.

MOUNT VERNON

The Future Is Now

Ind. 69 twists along the Ohio, past the giant General Electric complex before joining Ind. 62 on its route into Mount Vernon, the Posey County seat.

It has been almost 200 years since the first settlers made Mount Vernon their home. It has not, however, faded into history and its greatest growth appears to be ahead. New factories near town have brought new residents to the city of 7,500 in the last 25 years.

Above the river's edge, city workers repair a bandstand that marks the city's 175th birthday (1816-1991). Sunshine Park which surrounds the bandstand is a popular place, even before noon on a warm spring day.

Russell Bratcher stops to talk. He's a retired captain who piloted boats on the Ohio as well as the Mississippi "from St. Paul to New Orleans, the Illinois and Tennessee Rivers. Spent 37 years on boats, 33 as a captain. Retired in 1971," he says.

He is wearing a hat marked "Peerless Tavern." The bar is nearby at the corner of Water and Main, just a short distance from the Ohio. A man who has spent much of his life on the river wants to stay on the river.

A woman in a red convertible with the top down drives into the park and stops near the river. It's a good day to show her preschool-age granddaughter the sights.

Calvin Cox is at a swing with his two-year-old grandson, Seth, who seems happy with the attention. Cox, "born and raised in town," says Mount Vernon doesn't look like Mount Vernon anymore. "Old buildings have been torn down, some have burned, and new ones have gone up."

As he speaks, a giant piece of metal from the elevator smacks the ground, the noise reverberating along the river. The Mount Vernon Milling Company where Cox once worked is being demolished, another landmark on its way into history.

And Mount Vernon will look even different tomorrow than it does today.

WEST FRANKLIN

The Boerner Brothers

Mount Vernon is at the point of one of the Ohio's many horseshoe bends. We drive through the city on Ind. 62, past Southwind Maritime Center, southwestern Indiana's river port, and the big Bristol-Meyer Squibb Company plant.

We turn south on Lamont Road — another gravel surface — in search of a river town called West Franklin. The roads twist and turn, as does the river, south and east, along fields and woods.

We stop near a T intersection of unpaved roads in southeastern Posey County at a brick school, long abandoned as a place of learning.

Across the road two men are at work on a John Deere tractor, preparing for another farm season. They are Jim Boerner, the farmer, and his brother, Jerry, who is a retired Squibb employee.

"Ready for a big year?" we ask. They laugh for they know, as we do, that nothing in farming is certain.

They are pleasant, friendly, ready to talk about themselves and their ancestors. Both look across the road at the brick building. It was, they say, the West Franklin School, which opened in 1906, the year their father was born.

"That's where we got some of our education, such as it is," Jerry laughs.

The Boerner family has a long history in the area, dating back into the 1800s. A sign issued by the state, notes the farm where Jim lives has belonged to Boerners for more than a century.

Their grandfather, they relate, arrived in the area from Germany when he was 19, broke except for 50 cents that remained from the $6 he had on arrival in New York. Jim relates a story about the grandfather's first day in the area:

"He got here on a Sunday and stopped at a tavern to ask where he could find some friends who had arrived earlier. 'Just wait here,' the tavern keeper told him, 'because they always stop here after church.'

"Sure enough, his friends came to the tavern and my grandfather, the story goes, spent his last 50 cents on drinks for them."

Like most immigrants, he worked hard, saved his money and, according to his grandsons, bought farms for each of his eight children, four boys and four girls.

Times have changed since the first Boerner arrived. Smoke rises from the stacks at the Southern Indiana Gas & Electric Company's A. B. Brown power plant a half-mile or so away, generating electricity that wasn't then available.

(A few weeks after our visit high winds damaged the power plant, ripping apart one of the two cooling towers. The storm left much of Posey and neighboring Vanderburgh County without power.)

What is left of the town of West Franklin is hard against the Ohio. Houses at river's edge are elevated off the ground to avoid flood waters. A car has found a port under one of the homes that rests on stilts.

The town has a one-stop mail service, 11 boxes on one corner, each with a name. One of those names is Charlie Rohrbacher, a man the Boerners says knows the area better than anyone. It is unfortunate he is not at home.

West Franklin no longer has a store or retail business, just the homes and a "West Franklin" sign that keeps it on the map.

The Vanderburgh County line is a short distance to the east. We have finished our trip on the edges of Posey County. With Illinois to its west, Kentucky to its south, it has the longest state line border of any Indiana county.

VANDERBURGH COUNTY

One of state's smallest counties in size, its population of 167,000 one of the largest. Formed in 1818 and named for William Henry Vanderburgh, a Revolutionary War officer and an Indiana Territory Supreme Court judge.

DAM 48

A Rusty Reminder

We continue along the river after crossing from Posey County into Vanderburgh County at a point where Golden Rule Road meets Old Henderson Road.

Just off the river a rusted water tank overlooks a row of homes, some occupied, some vacant, at least one for sale. A marker on a

Old Dam 48 pump house in Vanderburgh County

brick building shows high water marks left by the river during floods.

We are in a ghost community. Two men cleaning debris from a vacant home explain the buildings once provided government housing for men who worked at old Dam 48 on the river. A two-story brick building that looks like a school, they say, was a pump house.

"Had something to do with the dam," one of the men says.

Dam 48, its purpose served, was no longer needed when new dams and locks were built on the Ohio in the mid-1900s. Like others that once helped control the river, it no longer exists, and the homes where its workers lived are now privately owned. It is a remote community whose past was brighter than its future.

HAPPE TIME

Mud in the Eye

Old Henderson Road follows the Ohio around a bow before it turns back north toward Evansville. Except for some houses on the river banks, the land varies from swamps to rich fertile fields.

Parts of the road are paved with concrete poured decades earlier to withstand floods. The L&N Railroad is elevated for miles on its route to the north, an engineering marvel from an earlier time.

Fields stretch out to the north as far as the eye can see, covering thousands of acres of farm land. Grain storage elevators are elevated on concrete piers, crossed with steel railings, to avoid high water when the Ohio leaves its banks.

The bottomland fields are divided by what are generously called roads. Happe Road, we soon learn, is not a wise choice for travel after a heavy rain. It is like driving on mush sprinkled with salt, the mush being the mud, the salt a scanty layer of gravel.

We are happy to leave Happe Road.

DOGTOWN TAVERN

Worth Hunting For

The Dogtown Tavern is a sanctuary for strangers, a popular dining spot for residents from nearby Evansville.

We find it at Old Henderson and Cypress Roads, the sign proclaiming, "Famous Susie Carr's Dogtown Country Style Cooking Restaurant. Open Monday through Saturday. Full menu 9 a.m. to 10:30 p.m. Closed on Sundays."

Susie Carr Scoles is the proprietor, has been since she took over the tavern from her parents in 1981.

So why is it called the Dogtown Tavern? The Cypress Saloon, so goes the legend, was renamed "Dogtown Tavern" by local residents who once had to walk through packs of hunting dogs to enter the place. The dog owners were inside slaking their thirst and feeding their hunger after a day in the woods, fields and river banks nearby,

Dogtown is not just a tavern, or a restaurant. It's an institution. The building, often flooded, was built sometime prior to 1889 to house the Cypress Post Office and saloon.

Dogtown Tavern southwest of Evansville

When the post office closed in 1915, the saloon expanded into the vacated area.

The tavern, indeed, looks to be a century old. Ancient belt-driven fans hang from high ceilings. The tables are vinyl covered, the floor terrazzo. The tavern section seats 73, the dining room 90.

This is a friendly place. Kate Carr, who ran the tavern with her husband from 1950 to 1981, is here on this date. She has brought an employee the German chocolate cake she baked and decorated with "Happy Birthday Debbie."

Mrs. Carr recalls the flood of 1964 when the river covered the tavern floor with 18 inches of water. "But that was mild compared to the depth of the big 1937 flood," she says, pointing to a mark higher on the wall.

It is the atmosphere and the menu that bring lawyers and business executives to Dogtown. Prices are reasonable, the fare varied, chicken, beef, pork and seafood. A 12-ounce choice ribeye, for example, is $12.95, a ten ounce filet $11.95. A char-broiled, marinated boneless/skinless chicken breast on a bed of broccoli with cheese sauce and potato wedges is $8.95.

No one who enters hungry leaves that way. The previously uninformed departs with a sense of history and an appreciation of life down on the river.

EVANSVILLE

Riverside City

Old Henderson Road leads north along the river into Evansville, Indiana's third largest city (behind Indianapolis and Fort Wayne), with a population of 127,000.

It is a city of diversified industry and commerce, the county seat of Vanderburgh County and a shopping center for southwestern Indiana, northern Kentucky and southeastern Illinois.

Evansville, has used its location on the Ohio for transportation and for recreation. Its waterfront at the Riverside Historic District is an attraction for residents as well as visitors.

Riverfront Park, which extends for a half-mile high above a boat dock, offers an expansive view of the river from the top of its horseshoe bend.

A man, more interested in the pursuit than the catch, has three fishing lines in the water. Pleasure boats are on the river. Two barges ply the water, one headed downstream, one upstream.

The Ohio narrows to 850 feet before it makes the bend to the south, creating an ominous obstacle for ship captains. Swift currents at times cause the towboats to perform a controlled slide around the bend, leaving the stern only a few hundred feet off Riverfront Park. High-powered towboats with twin turbo engines aren't easy to maneuver when pushing 15 barges loaded with grain, steel or crushed stone.

Couples speak as they stroll the 20-feet-wide walk next to Riverside Drive. Some stop to talk. Hoosier hospitality is alive and well. A couple, down from Michigan for an annual visit, relaxes on the waterfront, a picture post card for the tourism bureau.

Chris Robinson is enjoying the afternoon sun on the river. He has traveled over most of Indiana and visited Evansville often before moving from Princeton six months earlier. He likes the town.

"People around here are a lot more calmer, a lot less violent, than they are in cities up north. People in Gary and some other cities want to live life in a fast lane. Down here, people want to mellow out."

But he's not entirely happy. "I don't know what to think about Evansville. I don't like what they are doing to the landscape.

They're destroying nature, destroying everything. I remember when there was grassland and trees along the river.

"I'm 30 and I've been on this walkway off and on since I was about five. I remember how it once was and I just don't like for them to tear it up. God put it here for a reason and we're just tearing it up."

It is a short time before state-approved gambling is due in the city. Robinson seems to contradict himself. "I'm waiting for the riverboat casino to come and bring more business and more jobs." And chances are more change in the Evansville he has known since he was five.

At a high-rise apartment at Sycamore and Riverside, a man sits on his balcony viewing the area. Chances are he, too, likes Evansville the way it is.

At the east end of the park, a ten-foot-tall statue, two soldiers helping a wounded comrade, stands at the entrance to the Four Freedoms Memorial.

Flags of all branches of the military fly near the statue, a Korean War memorial for all services sponsored by veterans of C Company, 16th Infantry Battalion, U.S. Marine Corps.

It is a reminder that 54,246 Americans were killed, 103,284 wounded in what has become known as the Forgotten War.

Stone markers representing each state with the date they entered the nation ring the Four Freedoms columns made of native limestone. The stone base, 75 feet in diameter, represents the union of states, the 13 steps the original colonies. A restoration committee began a fund drive in 1995 to help restore the Four Freedoms (freedom from fear, freedom of speech, freedom from oppression, freedom of religion) monument.

Up river past nice homes, many of which are three story reminders of a more elegant time, is the Museum of Arts and Science, one of many cultural attractions in the city.

Like most river towns, Evansville's history is long, its land-marks many, its points of interest enough for a week's visit.

ANGEL MOUNDS

An Indian Village

Green River Road is off the I-164 expressway toward the Ohio where roads lead through farm fields and past houses at the river edge.

We wind our way to Pollack Avenue and past a residential community to the Angel Mounds State Historic Site.

The 500-acre park is the site of a Middle Mississippi Indian Village occupied between 1200 and 1400. The village included eleven man-made platform mounds, a town plaza and a village area for a thousand residents.

Excavated by the Indiana Historical Society, Angel Mounds on this spring day appears unkempt and in need of more attention by the Division of State Parks.

East of Angel Mounds in Warrick County is Newburgh, which is almost a continuation of Evansville.

Along the Ohio

WARRICK COUNTY

Named for Capt. Jacob Warrick, a hero of the Battle of Tippecanoe. Established 1813, three years before Indiana became a state. Population 46,000. County seat at Boonville. Contrasting terrain, rich bottomland, rolling pastures, hilly upland. Giant Aluminum Company of America plant at Yankeetown.

NEWBURGH

Worth A Toot

Newburgh appears to remain in a time lock and that is its charm. Not far from Evansville across the Vanderburgh County line in Warrick County on Ind. 662, it is a town of well kept older homes above a picturesque water front.

It is one of the state's oldest towns and its history is reflected in buildings preserved from the 19th Century.

The site where Maj. John Sprinkle set foot in 1803 to establish the first permanent settlement in Warrick County is marked. Sprinkle, a blacksmith from Pennsylvania, later laid out the town of Sprinklesburg which became Newburgh in 1837.

Newburgh claims it was the first town north of the Mason-Dixon line to be captured by Confederate forces, but it likely wasn't as dramatic as tourism pamphlets portray. Gen. Adam R. Johnson with a guerrilla band crossed the Ohio River on July 18, 1862, and confiscated ammunition and supplies without a shot being fired.

No matter! It was enough to merit a historical marker and add a page to the proud history of the town. Plaques placed by the

Scene on street to Ohio River in Newburgh

Newburgh Women's Club are numerous, making a walking tour an informative trip back in time.

The plaques are posted, for example, at Town Hall, which was the Cumberland Presbyterian Church from 1853 to 1966, at private homes, at the Exchange Hotel, built in 1841, expanded in 1853 and used as a Civil War armory and hospital.

A tour of Newburgh complete, it is time for lunch. And what better place to dine than in the Princess Theater, an 80-year-old landmark down by the river now known as "Tootietown?"

Tootie's Coffee Shop, decorated in French country blue, offers a panoramic view of the river, including outside dining on the balcony in warm weather. The lunch menu is varied, from Belguim waffles to assorted sandwiches and soups.

The theater building is the new home for Angie Sinclair's Tootie Tittlemouse, a character who now appears in at least four colorfully illustrated children's books.

That's Newburgh, as old as yesterday, as new as tomorrow's best seller.

LaBELLE RIVIERE
"Beautiful River"

East of Newburgh, a marker reads: "You are overlooking a river that once belonged to France. While the name Ohio comes from an Iroquois word, in France it was LaBelle Riviere, 'a beautiful river.'"

Who are we to argue with the French. Besides, on this day, with the sun on its smooth water, the Ohio is a beautiful river.

The Newburgh Locks and Dam are upstream, another step in the rise of the Ohio. The elevation now is 358 feet, 16 feet higher than at Uniontown. Here, too, are parking spaces, picnic areas and a viewing location for visitors.

Up river off Ind. 66, is the giant Aluminum Company of America plant that has been an important part of Warrick County's economy for 40 years.

YANKEETOWN
Watts Happening

Jim Watts is at work at Yankeetown Food & Stuff, the only retail outlet in Yankeetown, a hamlet south of Ind. 66 said to be named by relatives of Ralph Waldo Emerson.

Watts and his wife Helen came across the Ohio from Kentucky to open the store 17 years ago. "We — me and my wife — own the store. And Kimberly there works for us," he says, careful not to slight an employee.

He calls Yankeetown "a small country town. I'd say people here are more friendly, more outgoing than in bigger cities.

"Most of our customers come in pretty regular so that makes it easier to get to know them. The area in general has a nice bunch of people," he adds. Unfortunately, few places have all nice people.

"Food & Stuff" is a convenience store, but it is a popular eating place, especially for workers at the ALCOA plant.

"We serve breakfast and feed about 35 customers at lunch," Watts adds. "We're kind of a convenience store but we mainly rely on our deli for sales."

Hats, baseball type, are big in southern Indiana. Watts has dozens of them on display in the store. "It (the hat collection) kind of started out," Watts explains, "when a supplier gave me one of his hats. Then the competition did the same thing. Then people started bringing hats to me. Now anyone who has a business with its name on a hat wants it on display here."

"Food & Stuff" is open from 6 a.m. to 5 p.m. Entrepreneurship in a small town requires long hours, but Jim Watt doesn't seem to mind.

As in many small towns, the newest building in Yankeetown appears to be the Volunteer Fire Department.

The old Yankeetown High School is now part of the Boonville consolidation, but basketball fans still recall back 50 years ago when its teams often scored in the 100s in one memorable season.

South out of Yankeetown, the pavement ends at a bridge over Little Pigeon Creek as it meanders toward the Ohio. Boaters are warned to use extreme caution when entering the Ohio River because of barge traffic.

East of Ind. 66, the Little Pigeon separates Warrick from Spencer County.

SPENCER COUNTY

Established 1818, population about 20,000. Named after Capt. Spier Spencer, a unit commander who died during the Battle of Tippecanoe. Abraham Lincoln's home county. Some small factories, but primarily an agricultural area.

HATFIELD
But No McCoy

Ind. 66, at times lined with fields, at times with woodland, continues to follow the course of the river in Spencer County.

Hatfield, population 900, is one of the county's largest towns. Duffy's Diner, a gathering spot for men, is open. So is the branch bank, the Hatfield Market and a few other businesses.

A general store in what was once the Oddfellows Lodge is closed. The lodge, built in 1912, is no longer in use, its windows now boarded.

At the edge of town, a man helps his son fly a kite in an open field. The father appears to be enjoying the experience more than the son.

EUREKA
And Other Surprises

We pass through a place called Eureka in an attempt to reach the Ohio which again turns south. There are no businesses, no retail outlets. The Eureka Masonic Lodge has taken over what once was the community's general store.

To the south are oil wells and storage tanks. The road leads past an abandoned one-room school to the French Island Marina and Boat Club. Some homes along the river, which Kentucky claims to the Indiana bank, appear to be year-round residences.

We return to County Road 200 South, the pavement funded, a sign says by the Community Economic Development Income Tax, which has given Indiana counties a new revenue source.

Away from the river, nice homes sit on hills with manicured lawns. One house is ringed by a board fence enclosing a grove of big beech trees. The land is rolling, the pastures green with grass for beef cattle.

At U.S. 231, we drive south to the Ohio bridge — painted Kentucky blue — into Owensboro one of the bigger cities between Louisville and Evansville. It is a shopping center for many residents of Spencer and other Indiana river counties.

This loop of the Ohio takes the border of Indiana almost as far south as it was at the Uniontown locks. Back in Indiana, we turn east off U.S. 231 onto Ind. 45 south of Patronville. A wooded subdivision, its lots on hills, is not far from the Ohio.

A side road off Ind. 45 southwest of Rockport leads to a splendid view of the Ohio for a long distance in each direction. It is a vista not found on tourist maps.

ROCKPORT
History and Intrigue

Home on bluff above river in Rockport

Had there been no Abe Lincoln there would still be a Rockport. Lincoln lore just adds to the heritage that belongs to the historic Spencer County seat.

Rockport couldn't be better named. The town of 2,300 is built on a rock ledge overlooking the Ohio far below.

To view Rockport, it is best to take the one-way road that drops sharply down the cliff and winds around Rocky Side Park. The bluff rises 100 feet over the river's edge where the first Rockport settlers lived in a shallow cave-like alcove in 1808.

It was from the river's bank that the 19-year-old Lincoln departed from his home to the north on his first flat boat trip to New Orleans. It was a journey where the future president saw slaves sold, a practice he vowed to stop if given the opportunity.

Lincoln left for Illinois a short time later, but he returned in 1844 to speak at the Spencer County Courthouse in support of Henry Clay, the Whig Presidential candidate.

Rockport is a good stop for those who seek mystery and intrigue as well as history.

Above the bluff is the Sharp House, built about 1867, by Mathias and Katherine Sharp on property once owned by Judge John Pitcher, a friend of Lincoln. Designed by an architect, it was the first bluff house to be built with the front facing the river.

A nice house, however, did not make for a happy home. Mathias Sharp died in the house from poisoning as did Katherine's second husband.

She was prosecuted for the poisoning. A marker at the house adds, "Some believe the ghosts of the two men still inhabit the house." If true, the ghosts couldn't ask for a better view for houses on the ridge offer a magnificent view of the Ohio.

Up river on Ind. 66 from Rockport is an Indiana Michigan Power Company plant, its towers rising high over the river. Generating stations are not scenic, but Hoosiers along the Ohio accept this blend of commerce and nature.

GRANDVIEW
Life and Death

Ind. 66 borders the Ohio from Rockport to Grandview, another town aptly named for the view of the river here is indeed grand.

It is here at the park on the bend of the Ohio that visitors can relax, enjoy the scenery and, in season, gather nuts from under the pecan trees.

It is peaceful and serene; quiet, too, as are most towns of 700. But that doesn't mean a fellow can't get disgusted now and then. Take Abe Lincoln, for example.

A marker at the Grandview branch of the Spencer County library, notes that Lincoln traveled through town behind an oxen team pulling wood for barrels to the Ohio.

Legend has it that Lincoln became miffed when he was not invited to attend festivities following the wedding of Elizabeth Ray and Reuben Grigsby and another couple.

Age 20 at the time, Abe, perhaps in retaliation, satirized the event in a composition, "The Chronicles of Reuben." Written in Biblical style, the story relates how the two grooms mistook their respective brides in the Grigsby house and almost spent the wedding night with the wrong wife.

A publisher today could make a fortune with a book like that written by a would-be president.

Not all is happiness on this day, either. A long funeral caravan creeps its way to the town cemetery on a knoll a half-mile or so from the river.

Each resident of small towns is important. And no one is buried without proper respects. But life goes on, as it has for nearly two centuries, on this idyllic spot on the Ohio.

FERRY PARK

Lincoln the Ferryman

Not every step Lincoln took in Spencer County is marked, but no one complains that many of them are noted.

Ferry Park at the west edge of the county offers a panoramic view up river to Tell City and Cannelton from its shelter house.

The park is on the Anderson River which separates Spencer from Perry County. It was here, where the river flows into the Ohio, that the Lincoln family is said to have stopped before settling to the northwest.

Lincoln worked for a time about 1825 as a ferryman on the Anderson River and it was at the river junction his family shipped its farm produce.

PERRY COUNTY

Established 1814, current population about 19,200. Named for Commodore Oliver H. Perry who forced the British to surrender a squadron of ships in 1813 on Lake Erie. Half the acreage is wooded and much of it belongs to the Hoosier National Forest.

TROY

Standing Watch

Almost every town has its own niche, something that sets it aside, gives its residents pride.

Troy is, as the welcome sign proclaims, "The Gateway to Perry County." And a scenic gateway it is. Not far from the Anderson River, Troy was once the county seat and an important river town where early homes were built of sandstone quarried from the hills to the north.

It also has played a role in the religious life of the area. Overlooking the town is the St. Pius V Roman Catholic Church, built more than a century ago, its spire rising 142 feet. It was from Troy, the Rev. Joseph Kundek traveled north to establish parishes at Fulda and Ferdinand en route to Jasper.

On a hill above the town is the 18-foot "Christ of the Ohio" monument, standing watch, a silent message of peace and a guide to pilots and rivermen on the Ohio. It was sculpted by Herbert Jogerst, a German who came to America after World War II, took a job at nearby St. Meinrad seminary and was commissioned to design the statue.

Its boom days as a river town have passed, but 500 or so residents still call Troy home. As we mentioned in the book *Backroads Indiana*, it is a scenic stop, a quiet place to pause and listen . . . and visualize a time faded in history.

TELL CITY

Pretzels and Pride

It is early morning, a week day, and the Tell Street Cafe is busy. Most of the seats at a table for 12 are filled, men and women enjoying each other's stories.

It is not an exclusive group. When one person leaves, another enters to take his chair. It is an exchange of news and commentary that would rival a radio talk show.

The food is good. Local residents don't frequent places where it isn't.

No one should visit the town without stopping at the Tell City Pretzel Company, an institution here since 1858. That was when Casper Gloor a master baker from Switzerland opened his store and used a secret recipe from his native Switzerland to make the pretzels which became famous in the new community.

Gloor died in 1912, leaving the recipe to employee Alex Kessler, who passed it on to his two sons. Even now, the pretzels are still hand twisted and baked in the old-fashioned manner that gives them quality and taste which account for their wide acceptance.

The pretzels may be bought at the store or ordered for home delivery.

Compared to its neighbor Troy and other river towns, Tell City has a short history. Casper Gloor and other members of the Swiss Colonization Society bought 4,154 acres in 1856 and designated it in honor of the legendary Swiss hero, William Tell.

Tell City never reached the size its founders expected, but it did grow to become Perry County's biggest city (7,500).

Besides pretzels, Tell City is known for its fine furniture and its flood wall, a 20-feet high wall of concrete built to protect the community after the river's disastrous rampage in 1937.

It is also the Perry County seat of government, the offices being moved here in 1994 from nearby Cannelton. It was laid out originally to be the county seat, which explains why the 100-year-old three-story City Hall is in the center of a block which is the hub of the city.

Bill Goffinet is mayor of Tell City. He's also one of its biggest boosters. And he is willing to talk, just as soon as he finishes a phone call.

Meantime, his secretary, Debby Beavin, back from the second of two winter trips to Florida, shares her pride in the area: "I've been to a lot of different places and to a lot of different states and I wouldn't trade this for any of them. I think Perry is the most gorgeous county there is. There are so many good things even the people who live here don't realize what we have.

"Last summer we did a lot of biking and trail walking. We found places here that we did not know existed—cliffs and rocks and streams which absolutely beautiful if you take the time to find them."

It is 8:30 a.m. but Mayor Goffinet has been at work for some time. His desk is lined with letters to answer, memos of phone messages, but he is eager to promote his city.

"It is one of the prettiest parts of the state. A lot of people talk about Brown County, but in Perry we have the hills and trees and a tremendous amount of recreational opportunities.

"The Calumet Region has the lake. We have the Ohio River, the locks and dams up river, which afford a lot of opportunity for us . . . fishing and bass tournaments.

"Our industrial climate here is so much different than in northern Indiana. Where it has a lot of steel mills and huge industries, we have woodworking industries and a General Electric plant. Ours is a more quiet type of industry," he adds.

Life styles are different too. "It is a quieter, simpler life than in the north," the mayor says.

There are few ethnic differences in Tell City, a majority of residents are of French and German heritage even though it was settled by Swiss and named after Swiss hero William Tell.

"My ancestors came from Belgium," the mayor explains, and adds, "We don't, however, have as many different groups as in bigger cities."

Rebuilt Ind. 37 which linked Tell City to Interstate 64 has helped attract new industry. Perfect Fit Industries opened a plant here in 1995 which will eventually employ 300 workers in the production of pillows.

"It is a clean industry that sits out in a rural area and has the rural surroundings people seem to like," the mayor adds. He apparently is correct.

A few weeks after our visit, it was revealed that Waupaca Foundry, a Wisconsin firm, would build a $55 million casting facility near Tell City.

Goffinet makes no secret about his pride in Tell City. "I was born and raised here in the county. This is home," eying the work piled on his desk.

It is time for him to get on with the business of being mayor.

TRAVELERS' WARNING

Tourists on Ind. 66 are advised that motels are few and restaurants sometimes difficult to locate. Bed and breakfasts are more numerous than motels in small towns and cities.

After a long day, the Day's Inn in Tell City is a welcome stop, the first motel in miles.

The Patio Steak House between Tell City and Cannelton on Ind. 66 is an unexpected pleasure in dining, the menu varied, the food good, the atmosphere pleasant.

CANNELTON

Lost in Time

A sign on Ind. 66 proclaims, "The People of Cannelton Welcome You." And they do, at places like Yaggi's Bar, a popular gathering spot, and at other businesses in this historic town on the Ohio.

Oh, a few residents may still lament the loss of the county seat to Cannelton, but most have accepted what is too late to change.

And, anyhow, the old sandstone Courthouse is being taken over by Historic Cannelton Inc. and may be converted for use as a museum and for offices for the city of Cannelton.

And Cannelton is a city, one of the state's smallest with a population of 1,750. It is a city that has retained many of its older buildings and its historic business district.

This is a city best observed on foot, leisurely, for there is much to see.

North of Ind. 66, the main thoroughfare, a spire rises 156 feet over St. Michael's Roman Catholic Church, completed in 1859 by the city's German Catholics. The Episcopal Church, a few blocks south, was built in 1845.

To the south is Cannelton High School, still in use as it has been since 1922 despite the trend toward consolidation. Its Bulldog basketball teams have played in the same gymnasium since 1924. With 111 students (as of 1995-96) it is one of the three smallest public high schools in the state.

Visitors to the downtown district step back in time. Buildings remain from an earlier time, some dating back to the mid-1880s. Most have second floors for they were built when merchants lived above their businesses.

The Cannelton Cotton Mill, a three-story 150-year-old sandstone structure covering an entire block, remains vacant. It ceased operation in 1954 and efforts to reopen it for different uses have failed. Its iron fire escapes and doors have been repainted and it is good to see that some effort has been made to repair the landmark.

* * *

Perry County doesn't have a tourism director, but it has promoters like Mayor Bill Goffinet and Karen Stonewall.

Stonewall is the district solid waste director, working from an office in the Cannelton City Hall at the east edge of town.

"It is a wonderful community to live in, and it has so many good things to offer," she boasts. "About 23 percent of the land in the county is owned by the Hoosier National Forest, so we have a lot of woodland. With the trees and 17 access points to the river, the county is a prime location for tourists."

She is too convincing to doubt. Bob Cummings would have been proud of her. Cummings, who was editor of the Cannelton News until his death in 1971, was an early promoter of the county's attractions. The Lincoln Trail Bridge that crosses the Ohio east of Cannelton is named in his memory.

BARGES AND BOATS

Lafayette Was Here

The Cannelton Locks and Dams a short distance up river may be viewed from an observation area three flights above ground. A pilot eases hundreds of tons of cargo — three barges wide, five barges and 1,100 feet long — through the locks, waiting to be lowered 25 feet on its slow journey down river.

There are only inches to spare. The captain, we decide, is a better driver than motorists who wheel power-steered cars over the twists and turns of Ind. 66.

The Lafayette Springs rest stop marks the area where the Marquis de Lafayette came ashore May 9, 1825, after the steamboat Mechanic sank after hitting a submerged ledge of an island. A passing craft picked up the men the next morning.

Rock outcroppings form a ledge on the north side, almost creating a retaining wall as Ind. 66 rises with the hills, then drops quickly to the river's banks. At times, the route is near the river, separated by guard rails, leaving little room for driver error.

We reach Rocky Point, a junction of Ind. 66 and Ind 166. It is here that Little Deer, Middle Deer and East Deer Creeks empty into the river. The Rocky Point Marina is a busy recreation center.

TOBINSPORT

Fire, Flood, Disaster

Shock absorbers were made for cars driving the six miles from Rocky Point to Tobinsport over Ind. 166. The road rises and falls, the pavement uneven, a roller coaster ride at river's edge at no extra charge.

This is another of Indiana's peninsulas, the Ohio forming a bend south to the deepest point of the state up river from Owensboro.

A small lake formed by Ohio bayous is home to weekend campers. A cemetery next to the Clayton Harris Memorial United Methodist Church reflects the past and present, tombstones for settlers, newer graves for men and women who have died in the 1990s.

Ind. 166 ends at the river next to a house and trailer marked emphatically with two "Private Property — Keep Out" signs. It is the site of a former state boat ramp, since abandoned.

Tobinsport, in the days before cars, was a river port, a much busier place than it is today. Little remains, the high school is gone, so are the stores. Fewer than 20 homes remain.

A man working on a truck points east to the site of the old Tobinsport High School across from the Gilead Church American Baptist. "The school burned, so did the store which housed the post office," he tells us.

Fire and flood have taken their tolls on Tobinsport, leaving its role in the development of the state lost in history books.

There are few roads in this tip of Indiana and we retrace our route on Ind. 166 to a sign at Millstone Road that points to "Kiwanis Electra Park."

A mile to the east a monument marks the site where a Northwest Airlines Lockheed Electra turbojet crashed on March 17, 1960. Names of the crew and passengers are engraved on the stone in the one-time soybean field.

The monument was financed by the Cannelton Kiwanis Club through public subscriptions "in the hope that such tragedies will be eliminated." A wilted bouquet remains on the base of the marker.

Out on the road a falcon loosens its grip on a smaller bird, leaving its prey on the pavement as a car approaches.

TWISTS AND TURNS
And Constant Surprises

East of Rocky Point, Ind. 66 follows the Ohio which has turned back north from Tobinsport. The road twists like a cow path, making a 90-degree turn around a farm house with an American flag flying on a pole. The route, hilly through a section of the Hoosier National Forest, passes the entrance to the German Ridge recreation area, quickly changes to rolling farm land. On a ridge a short distance ahead, through still bare trees, is another scenic view of the Ohio.

It is one of a series of almost constant surprises on the route, making it one of the most enjoyable roads in the state to drive.

As the pavement drops steeply over a hill into the lowland at river's edge, a car passes at a high speed despite the turns. It has a Kentucky license plate and the driver obviously is not interested in Indiana scenery. It is his loss.

ROME
Too Good to Lose

Old Perry County Courthouse in Rome

Rome, Zip Code 47574, is south of Ind. 66. At the post office we are greeted by Wanda Winchell, postmaster, volunteer fireman, fund raiser, community promoter and tourism director.

She is accustomed to visitors for Rome is a picture post card setting on a river's edge.

"We have people come here from everywhere. Folks like history and scenery," she explains. There is plenty of both with a slice of goodwill on the side.

She talks about her life as postmaster, a four-hour-a-day job she has held for 13 years. With twelve post office boxes, nine general delivery customers and 100 stops on a rural route, it's not a full-time position.

"It is just nothing like a big post office. Here you know everybody. It's the social center of town. I bought these chairs (white vinyl) so folks would have seats where they can sit and visit when they come for their mail."

She relates an experience to indicate she is more than a mail sorter and stamp seller. "It's just like Nola there. She was walking home this morning and the telephone rang. It was the doctor's office calling to see if Nola had picked up her mail. She had, but I let out a war whoop you could hear all across Rome. She heard me and came back and answered the phone. She doesn't have one of her own, you know.

"Here you are not just a postmaster, you are a friend of everybody," she adds.

Maybe that should be in the job description for all postmasters.

She turns from postmaster to community promoter. "We are close knit. People down here — those in Rome and those for miles around — are friendly. If anyone is in trouble and needs help, we all pitch in and do what we can for each other. The only way you can keep anything functioning — the community center, the lodge, the fire department, the church — is through volunteers."

Rome, though, she admits is still not paradise. "Like everywhere else, you have some great volunteers and some who are not so great."

The little postoffice is on a rounded corner within feet of a street. "The sounds of heavy machinery around the post office and the rumble of barges on the river are big events around here," she jokes.

That's Rome today. Quiet, friendly, serene. The Rome of the past was far different. Back in the 1800s and into the early 1900s there were houses all over the valley and down to the river.

"It was a thriving town," Mrs. Winchell says. "Two stores, three doctors, a saloon."

Rome once was the seat of Perry County. The two-story brick with a cupola on a hip roof, was built about 1820 and used as a courthouse until 1859 when Cannelton became the county seat. It was the Rome Academy from 1860 to 1867, a public school for decades, and now is the community center.

The town changed gradually, then dramatically, when the 1937 flood inundated much of the area. Farmers left the land, families moved to bigger towns and Rome was left to folks like Mrs. Winchell, who worry about more changes.

"Our fear is that the Postal Service will close small post offices like this. It already is closing some as postmasters retire."

Some post offices are not self-sustaining, she admits, but correctly adds, "Once you do away with the post office in rural areas, the towns lose their identities and pretty soon there is nothing left."

It would be regrettable if there were no more Romes.

REBELS WITH CAUSE
But No Sympathizers

Back on Ind. 66 the road rises in elevation once again, passing a farm house with a great view overlooking the river. Again the road drops sharply into a valley to a site of a Rebel incursion during the Civil War.

It was here on June 17, 1863, that Capt. Thomas Henry Hines and his 62 Confederate troops came into Indiana to recruit southern sympathizers. He did not succeed. The Home Guard captured most of the invaders on a river island above Leavenworth but Hines escaped.

DERBY
Doff of the Hat

Ind. 66 again meets the river southwest of Derby, a Perry County town built on a hill at the edge of the Ohio.

Postal service is a family affair in these parts. On duty at the Derby post office is postmaster Betty Whitehead, the sister of Wanda Winchell.

Betty was postmaster at Rome before she moved to Derby. Derby is bigger, the post office is open six hours a day and has more mail boxes to fill and more customers to serve. But it isn't the social center that the Rome post office is.

"The general store has more people in and out than we do, but we are sort of the messenger center for the community," Mrs. Whitehead explains.

"People call up to see if someone is here. Or they'll leave a message knowing someone will be in here. Everybody looks after everyone else. People are very friendly around here. They know each other on a first name basis."

It is a town where the general store, a brown derby painted on its side, serves meals to the bereaved following funerals.

Despite deaths, Derby seems to be growing. New families, seeking a more peaceful life style, have moved here from places like Zionsville, Indianapolis and Bedford.

MAGNET

Worth a Hoot

We continue on Ind. 66 as it zigzags northeast through what is left of the community of Dexter, then take an unmarked Perry County road that meanders nearer the river into Magnet.

Another historical marker is at the river road entrance into Magnet from the south. It notes the location where the steamer U.S.S. Argosy, caught in storms, blew aground when her boilers exploded August 21, 1865. Ten Union soldiers, who had survived the Civil War, perished on their way home in the disaster. All were buried in a mass grave near the memorial marker.

Not much remains in Magnet, a couple of houses, a store and Hooter's Bar and Grill which — with the scenery and the peaceful surroundings — attracts people to town. It has done that on this day at noon. It is a good place to eat and watch the peaceful river, maybe see some barges ply the waters.

It is a favorite stop on each trip along the Ohio. It is a place for easy conversation, where pretense is as off limits as suits and ties.

A man returns from the men's room, a smile on his face. It is obvious he has read the sign left by the custodian above the stool: "My aim is to keep this bathroom clean. Your aim will help."

Three adults and a college student are at the restaurant at mid-day, having lunch before driving on up to Buzzard Roost, an observation point high above the river.

The Perry-Spencer Bookmobile has made its Magnet stop and the driver and librarian are at lunch, too. The big Blue Bird van, they say, carries more than 5,000 titles as it traverses Perry and Spencer Counties.

Pat Irwin is the waitress, bartender and cook. She's busy, but still friendly, still liking the job that has been hers for almost two decades.

Hooter's is much busier at night, especially on Fridays and Saturdays when diners drive for miles to enjoy the food and end the isolation that has kept them away for a week.

We will soon be leaving Perry County. The southeast section of Crawford County awaits.

CRAWFORD COUNTY

Established 1818, population about 10,000. Named after Col. William Crawford, a surveyor and close friend of George Washington. Large sections of the county have become parts of the Hoosier National Forest. Only the southeast section of the county borders the Ohio.

BUZZARD ROOST
Theater of the Mind

A frequent visitor to Buzzard Roost has mixed emotions about the new pavement on the route. It is easier to drive, but it may be more inviting to others to seek the beauty of the views ahead. It has, in the past, been the isolation that has added to the area's charm.

Perry County ends, Crawford County begins where the Ohio turns softly east from its northerly direction. The road runs high above the winding river, unveiling a panoramic view of the Kentucky valley on the opposite side. Tulip poplars line the road, unscathed by chain saws.

It is still early spring and the trees have not leafed, leaving openings to the river below. Unfortunately there are no good spots to pull off the road and appreciate the scenic overlook. That changes, however, when a side road leads to Buzzard Roost Overlook, seven-tenths of a mile off the Magnet-Alton Road. It is an awesome view from the small park which is elevated 400 to 500 feet above the river. Only a small strip of trees down at water's edge separate the bluff from the river, which is bluish-green as it reflects the sun.

It is quiet, the silence broken only by the muffled noise of a towboat, its engine on idle as it pushes barges down stream. It is possible, in the solitude, to think back to an earlier time, back to the days when a slaughter house was down on the river and the buzzards, feathered garbage disposers, gathered at night to scavenge the refuse of a day's butchering.

The skies are clear. Upstream around the slight bend of the river is Alton, an Indiana town down at water's edge. It is a panoramic view worth recording in the theater of the mind for replay later.

ALTON

Reasonable But Remote

We return to the Magnet-Alton Road which continues to rise, even higher above the river. Suddenly the pavement ends, only broken asphalt and crushed stone are ahead.

A small sign on a tree points to Alton, another Indiana secret worth seeing again. The road leads past small farms where tobacco seeds are germinating in hot beds heated by the day's sun.

The pavement begins again as the road starts its decline, offering another priceless view of the remote village below. Alton's elevation is 407 feet, a sharp contrast to the 875 feet a few miles back at Buzzard Roost.

A hand-made "Kids At Play" sign greets visitors to Alton. Another hand-crafted greeting offers a "Happy Birthday to Jack." There is little activity here. An attempt to start a store has apparently failed and the only retail outlet is a soft drink machine.

Most of the houses are in sharp contrast to an imposing structure with porches around the front and side of its two levels. It appears it could have been a hotel back when the river carried passengers instead of raw materials.

A "For Sale" sign is at the Crawford County Indian Museum, where artifacts had been on display. The museum, which had been the site of two annual festivals, has a restaurant and amphitheater. The listed price we are told is a reasonable $50,000, but the remoteness of Alton has hindered a quick sale.

We cross muddy Blue River just north of where it flows into the Ohio. The steel bridge is more than a century old, the single lane of its wooden floor lined with thick planks.

"No trespassing" signs block the entrance to a planned development east of Alton where roads wind around steep hills that unveil vistas along the river. The project seems to be at a standstill, possibly, again, because of Alton's remote location and unimproved roads.

OXBOW BEND
Where Kentucky is North

Northeast of Alton the road, now blacktop, again meets the river, guard rails protecting motorists from high bluffs with views to the water below. Again the Ohio makes a horseshoe bend forming a knob to the east.

Five miles from Alton, the road ends at a "T" intersection high above the river near what is called Artist's Point. A sign reads "Scenic Drive — Schooner's Point."

A home here offers what may be the best view in Indiana of the river and Kentucky beyond. We are greeted there by Melinda Koopman, her daughters, Rebecca and Roxanne, and their Great Dane, "Dutch."

It is a peaceful setting, one Mrs. Koopman has learned to enjoy over the last four years. Her husband, Ron, and his father built the house in 1984, planning to use it as a hunting cabin. When Ron and Melinda decided to make it their home, they doubled its size.

Melinda looks across the river. "That is Meade County, Kentucky," she explains. "It's the only place in Indiana where you can look north into Kentucky.

"We can look over there across and see how the season changes. That is really neat," she adds for emphasis.

The Koopman's place is "neat," too, thanks to Ron Koopman. "He keeps the area clean across the road. It wasn't that nice until he started caring for it," Melinda admits.

When you live on a bluff created by God and nature, you take care of it. And you don't mind when tourists stop by to appreciate for a few minutes what you can see year around.

We turn onto a road that follows the river closely around Oxbow Bend, the area of Indiana that extends like a horseshoe loop to a point called Cape Sandy. The road is a mixture of river gravel and broken asphalt as it follows the river and meanders through wooded areas to what is marked Schooner's Point. Ahead is a sandstone bluff, its rock sides reaching almost onto the narrow path, forcing cars even nearer a sharp drop off on the opposite side.

A number of farms, cattle grazing on lush grass, are at the end of the bow where a "Cape Sandy, Ind." sign is planted.

People out here like their privacy. The area is marked with no hunting and no trespassing signs. Ahead on the loop is Mulzer Crushed Stone Inc., a giant quarry covering a vast area along the river. It is here the stone is crushed, much of which is loaded onto barges for delivery up and down the Ohio. It is at Mulzer's where Ron Koopman works.

The drive around Oxbow Bend is ten miles, a trip worth the time.

FREDONIA

High and Dry

A sign points to Fredonia and Ind. 62. A number of houses, each with a view to the Ohio, are on the bluffs above Artist's Point.

Fredonia is one river town that never had to worry about floods. A benchmark here places the elevation at 670 feet compared to 410 down on the Ohio. It once, however, had a shipbuilding plant and a docking area for ships on the river.

The Crawford County seat was in Fredonia from 1822 to 1845 when it was moved inland to English. The town's Community Center was built to resemble the courthouse, a wall of which still stands.

What once was a general store is now a residence and no other retail outlets remain in Fredonia. It has been miles and hours since the last restaurant back at Magnet, longer still since we have seen a gasoline station.

LEAVENWORTH

The Risen Town

Above Fredonia, the tree-lined bluff opens to a wide lens view of Leavenworth, its Overlook Restaurant and water tower high above the river. The roadside, however, is too narrow to stop for a longer look at the Ohio as it makes a hairpin twist around Leavenworth.

"We Welcome You To Leavenworth — Building Our Riverfront Heritage," reads a sign on Ind. 62. In reality, there are two Leavenworths, the old down on the river, which was almost destroyed by the 1937 flood, the other high on the bluff where most of the town was relocated.

Some houses, street front homes, remain in the old section, close enough for the river to be a threat when the water rises. "The Dock" restaurant is open, but most other businesses have retreated to higher ground.

High above the river is the newer Leavenworth, developed over the last 60 years. The Leavenworth Town Hall is there, a center for area artists and craftsmen.

Nearby is Stevenson's "Old-Time" Store, an emporium filled with quality antiques and almost any item a person could want this side of metropolitan Louisville. The store, which also moved from down on the river, has operated for more than 75 years, its clerks as friendly as they were in the days when every town had a general store.

Diners who arrive early for lunch or dinner at the Overlook Restaurant are guaranteed great seats as well as good food. Window tables look upstream and down stream from the bend in the Ohio. Chances are at least one barge will pass during a meal.

The menu is varied, the atmosphere good, but on busy evenings waitresses and management may send unspoken signals that it is time to move on so other customers may be seated at your table. It is a view too good not to share with others.

We follow a county road up river from Leavenworth to the site of old Dam 44, which like Dam 48 near Evansville helped, at one time, to control the river. The two-story brick pump house remains, its lower half cluttered with graffiti. The site, we learn, is now owned by the town of Leavenworth which may permit a historical group to remodel the building for a museum.

East of the dam site, a giant barn is deteriorating. Houses are abandoned along this road which once was a main access into old Leavenworth. A road to the north crosses a small creek spanned by a wooden bridge with a plank floor and weakened guard rails.

We are back on Ind. 62 which follows the river, then passes through a section of the Crawford-Harrison State Forest, a 24,000 acre preserve which includes the Wyandotte Cave recreation area. The forest extends to the river which makes a long turn to the south from Leavenworth. No roads lead to the river in this rugged, wooded area of the state.

Near the county line, a barn roof reads, "Mail Pouch Tobacco — Treat Yourself to the Best." It is a fading form of advertising.

HARRISON COUNTY

Named for William Henry Harrison, governor of the Indiana Territory who later became the nation's president. One of the state's oldest counties, being established in 1818. First state capitol was at Corydon, the county seat. Population 30,000. Mostly agriculture in river bottoms.

LICKFORD

Buffaloes Roam

Seeking an access to the river, we take Ind. 135 south of Ind. 62 to a sign pointing west to "Lickford."

Buffaloes graze on a hillside not far from farm houses, some of which appear to have been built when the state was young. The terrain changes to steep hills and deep hollows before the road leads down a sharp incline to a place identified as "Lickford Camp Grounds."

This is the Lickford the sign pointed to, not a town as we expected.

An old steel bridge spans Indian Creek. Lickford Bridge Road leads past an abandoned farm to the river where a "Property of Kosmos Cement" sign is posted. A lone car, possibly parked by a mushroom hunter, is the only sign of civilization here along river's edge.

A Harrison County map shows roads leading south along the river toward New Amsterdam. There is no traffic, no houses for several miles, only cattle grazing near an opening to the river.

We stop at Harrison County's version of a shoe tree. Dozens of pairs of shoes, knotted at the laces, are lodged in the limbs of a tree

"Shoe tree" on road near New Amsterdam

at the edge of the road. It's a diversion, probably started as a prank, that has become a custom and may become a tourist attraction.

A car approaches, its driver waves as he passes. We are not alone!

NEW AMSTERDAM
Struggle for Survival

We reach New Amsterdam. The New Amsterdam store, a small red building, which had been in operation a couple of years ago on a previous visit, is closed. There are not enough residents to support a retail outlet or post office.

New Amsterdam is believed to be the smallest incorporated town in the state, its population 40 or so, depending on who's visiting and who's on vacation.

It wasn't always that way. It once was a busier town, with commerce and activity back when it was a stop for Ohio River traffic. An older general store, built on stone pillars to avoid flooding, closed years earlier, but a Camels cigarette sign and a "No Trespassing" warning remain. An American flag flies over an abandoned garage.

New Amsterdam never recovered from the 1937 flood. It now struggles to survive the loss of its high school, its post office, its businesses and most of its past.

A bridge is out at the edge of town, has been for years, never replaced by the town or the county. A smaller bridge, built by a property owner, is marked "Private Property — Cross at Your Own Risk." We have no choice for we want to stay close to the river en route to Mauckport. We cross the bridge and wave at a man splitting wood in a yard on the opposite side. He returns our greeting, with forgiveness, if he is the property owner.

A RIVER DRIVE
En Route to Mauckport

South of New Amsterdam, the Indiana side of the river is near the water level, bluffs rising on the Kentucky side, a change in what has been the case down river. Hereford cattle graze in fields. Satellite dishes are common, this being an area without cable TV lines. A threshing machine sits under roof in a drive-through corn crib, a reminder of an earlier time when farms were small and combines unknown.

It is a narrow road, its bridges dangerous, concrete sides three feet high, memorials to engineering in the days when traffic was scarce and speeds slower.

The road, scenic in spring when dogwood and redbud bloom, colorful in the fall when leaves change, makes a "U" turn on a hill, crossing a culvert. The pavement hugs the water, wash outs shored up with riprap stone, near where the river turns back east.

A "No Dumping" sign has been ignored by those who have not appreciated the beauty around them.

A farmer waters a hot bed where seeds germinate into plants to be reset later in tobacco fields. A truck waits patiently on the narrow road for us to ease past, another example of friendliness of the area's residents.

MAUCKPORT
Awaiting a Rebirth

It is easy to imagine back to 1937 when river flooded the entire area and doomed Mauckport to decades of decline. It never recovered, but that may be changing.

Postmaster Linnea Breeden, who grew up in Mauckport, says nearby rural areas are attracting new residents, some from Louisville. The post office is busier now than it has been in years.

Work on a long planned marina began in April, 1995. And the town has a remote chance for one of the riverboat casinos planned for Indiana. That could bring hotels, restaurants and traffic to the town that is easily accessible to Hoosiers on Ind. 135 and over the Matthew Welsh bridge for Kentuckians.

The prospects have led speculators to buy property in and around town. There hasn't been so much excitement since before the Civil War when Mauckport was a busy river town with an underground railroad station. On this Friday afternoon, the town tavern has but two customers, but others are expected once the work day ends.

Windows have been removed and bricks are being salvaged from a two-story home that is a reminder of the days when Mauckport was a thriving river town.

We drive past the marina site, then up river on Ind. 11 before it turns north. The banks remain low on the Indiana side, high in Kentucky across from Brandenburg.

LACONIA

School For Sale

The red clay soil, which will be a contrast to the loam in northern Indiana, makes good grassland on rolling farms along the drive. Few roads lead off the highway toward the river, but we take some of them, getting new views of the Ohio.

Like hundreds of other small towns, Laconia has lost its high school, which is now for sale. "Price Reduced," reads the sign out front. Laconia hasn't been the same since consolidation sent its students to South Central High.

Three businesses do remain at the Ind. 11-North Tobacco Landing Road intersection, the only trading center for miles. At Laconia, we take Kittner Bottom Road to an isolated nipple of Indiana seldom visited by travelers, but we must return to Ind. 11 for no roads led up river from that point.

Northeast of Laconia, a road leads south past "Helen's Dolls — Repairing and Dressing Dolls," a remote business far from town. A woman who owns and runs her own business has the right to determine where it is located, even if it is off the beaten path.

The pavement turns to crushed stone as it continues south. A driver waves as he passes us in the dust as the road drops toward the river through rugged terrain. We have reached the end — or the start — of Ind. 111.

On the state highway is New Boston, the site of old U.S. Dam 43 and its locks and pump house. The pump house, its water tower nearby, is now private property. So are two identical brick homes, which might have been residences for workers. A Nehi Cola sign remains on a long-closed store.

Ahead on Ind. 111, the land level on each side, is Evans Landing, a community with a few houses and an access to the river. A cemetery on a hill is safe from floods. Upstream, the terrain changes again, bluffs with outcropping of rocks, rising high above the road.

The river once again turns north at Rosewood, a settlement with a few houses. Ind. 111 follows the same course past more houses, most of which are well maintained with green lawns. Beyond Rosewood the road again swings closer to the river, its banks dotted with homes, mostly well maintained.

It is a nice, leisurely drive, with little traffic, it being too early for workers in metropolitan Louisville to be en route home.

Ind. 111 passes the intersection of Ind. 211, which leads inland to the town of Elizabeth. A couple miles ahead is the old river town of Bridgeport, once known by the postmark Locust Point, but now only a dot on the road map.

Floyd County is around the bend of the Ohio. Ahead is what Hoosiers call "The Sunny Side of the Ohio" — the triple cities of New Albany, Clarksville and Jeffersonville.

FLOYD COUNTY

Geographically, one of Indiana's smallest counties. Formed in 1819. Believed to be named for Davis Floyd, who campaigned for the new county and was its first circuit court judge. Population 65,000.

NEW ALBANY
An Indiana Secret

The Sherman Minton Bridge dominates the skyline for motorists who approach New Albany from the west on Ind. 111. The graceful, twin-arched doubled-decked span is named for a New Albany resident who became a Supreme Court justice after serving as a U.S. senator.

The Robert E. Lee steamboat marker on Ind. 111 notes that the craft built at nearby Falling Run Creek in the mid-1800s defeated the Natchez in a race from New Orleans to St. Louis. The Lee covered the distance in 90 hours, a record for steamboats that still stands.

Overshadowed by Louisville, New Albany, population 37,000, is one of Indiana's best kept secrets, especially to Hoosiers who drive though the city on I-74 without stopping.

It's a historic river city founded in 1813, just downstream from the Falls of the Ohio. Its setting adds to its history, the river to the front, a series of hills known as The Knobs ringing it to the north.

Water Street, which runs outside the levee that protects the city, provides a panorama of the river and the Louisville skyline. A few residents live in the flood area, friendly folks like a man who, unable to keep his dogs from chasing a car, smiles, shakes his head and waves instead.

Jaycees River Front Park is busy on an April day, youths on the basketball court, adults watching the eternal flow of the river. An amphitheater, facing the river on the levee embankment, will be busy when the weather warms.

More than a dozen homes, each almost as old as New Albany, are in the Mansion Row Historic District on Main Street. Among them are the Scribner House, built in 1814 by Joel Scribner, a founder of the city, and the Culbertson Mansion State Memorial, which was the home of financier and dry goods merchant William S. Culbertson.

At Bank Street and Main six Roman columns remain on a building that was New Albany's first bank. The old Second Baptist Church, whose clock tower was used as a landmark by boat captains, is at Third and Main. The church, said to have been a way station on the Underground Railroad prior to the Civil War, has been used by an African-American congregation since 1889.

A number of the earlier buildings are now law and business offices or private homes. Most are well-maintained, reminders of a time when maids and butlers helped the wealthy become accustomed to opulent lifestyles.

The people of New Albany are far different today, members of the working class who look forward to Friday nights. It is 5:30 p.m. and a long line waits on the sidewalk in front of the South Side Inn. "Bar and Restaurant," the sign over the modest building reads.

A clerk at the Holiday Inn says, "The South Side Inn is always like that. But the food is good, worth the long wait," she adds. An hour later, a line remains. The wait is too long. We go elsewhere for a nondescript meal, returning the next morning to find the South Side Inn does not serve breakfast.

CLARK COUNTY

Established in 1801 as state's second county, only Knox being older. Named for Gen. George Rogers Clark. Population 88,000. Much of the county is bounded by the Ohio River as it flows from the northeast to southwest.

CLARKSVILLE
Falls of the Ohio

Silver Creek divides Floyd and Clark Counties as it flows toward the Ohio. But it is difficult to tell where New Albany ends and Clarksville begins.

Clarksville, founded in 1783, is considered the first American town in the Northwest Territory even though Vincennes was an earlier French settlement. It is a city that had its start in the bravery of young Americans.

Gen. Clark built a cabin here on a site that overlooked the Falls of the Ohio in 1803 after he and his troops were given 150,000 acres of land in the area in recognition of their capture of Kaskaskia, Cahokia and Vincennes from the British and Indians.

Other settlers arrived, using the river for transportation, then moved north later.

Clarksville trailed its two neighbors in population for years, but its 20,000 residents now make it almost as large as Jeffersonville.

The Falls, visible on this day because spring rains and high water have yet to come, is the only major natural obstruction in the Ohio River's 981-mile course from Pittsburgh to the Mississippi. The series of violent rapids, known as the falls, are created by an outcropping of limestone that spans the river, causing it to drop 26 feet in three miles.

The McAlpine Locks and Dam at Louisville is the only project on the Ohio that was located to provide passage around a natural barrier.

The Interpretative Center at the Falls of the Ohio, one of Indiana's newest parks, has brick walks financed by money raised by schools, individuals and businesses. The 350-million-year-old fossil beds in the falls are the largest exposed Devonian fossil beds in the world. Rock collecting is prohibited, but the staff allows visitors to explore the thousands of fossils that can be found in the 220-acre park.

It is a park for historians, geologists, naturalists. There is no playground equipment, no rides, and young people who come here usually are with a science class.

It is early on a Saturday and Frank Nagel is one of the few people at the park. He is here to use a pay phone, not to observe what nature has created. But he has time to talk.

"I just bought a car for $395," he says, adds details, talks about his family and about politicians "who think they know it all."

It is obvious no one remains a stranger long around Frank Nagel. He apologizes for not talking longer, but he has errands to run. Some days a man is just too busy to smell the roses or appreciate a 350-million-year-old fossil bed.

Near the falls a sign warns, "Leave fossil beds when you hear siren. Water subject to sudden rise and violent turbulence when gates open." The gates are insurance against floods and can be raised to allow the water to pour across the falls.

Three ducks waddle across Riverside Drive near nice luxury apartments with windows to the river and Louisville beyond. Down on the water, the Riverside Landing restaurant offers dining aboard ship.

JEFFERSONVILLE
Restoration City

Jeffersonville, population 22,500, is almost as old as Clarksville, its settlement begun in the mid-1780s when Fort Finney was built near where I-65 now crosses the Ohio.

Federal and Victorian style homes from an earlier era are on the waterfront. Many in the Historic District are being restored to the grandeur that marked an earlier, more ostentatious time.

A river overlook is under construction near the marina where boats are docked.

The Historic Landmarks Foundation of Indiana and Jeffersonville Main Street Inc. have offices in the Grisamore House, a brick double, built in 1837 as residences for businessmen brothers David and Wilson Grisamore.

At strike-closed Jeffboat, a few idle workers prepare breakfast on a grill. It is a labor dispute that will end by summer, allowing work to continue on the new riverboat casino for Evansville.

Nearby is the Howard Steamboat Museum, a big three-story brick with gabled roof that is one of Jeffersonville's attractions.

Boats have always been important in Jeffersonville. And its role as a river town was accentuated in the 1995 municipal primary when Democrats nominated Tom Galligan as their mayoral candidate. At that time, Galligan lived on a boat. He won the primary, was elected and took office January 1, 1996.

UTICA
Failure To Pay

As it has been since New Albany, the river is lined with development. Up river from Jeffersonville expensive apartments and new homes, many upscale, are near the water front off the road to Utica. A few older homes remain, creating a mixture of the past and the present.

Home development stops for an industrial area and the Clark Maritime Centre, another Indiana port which opened the area to commercial traffic on the Ohio.

Utica, almost hidden from the New Albany-Clarksville-Jeffersonville complex, sits on the banks of the Ohio, a quiet town away from its busier neighbors.

It is too small for fast food outlets, but the Riverside Restaurant is open. A few men, obviously regular customers, plan a visit to the funeral home to view a departed friend, talk about a fund raiser for a cancer victim, discuss the health of other residents. They call most customers who enter by first names.

A plat map of the Utica of 1850 is on a wall of the restaurant. So are some other historical pictures. At the entrance, are two 18 by 25 montages, each labeled "Utica Folks," pictures of townspeople with golfer Fuzzy Zoeller, Gov. Evan Bayh and other dignitaries.

Caught up in the atmosphere, we thoughtlessly walk out without paying our bill, or even leaving a tip. We are 30 miles away before we realize our transgression. We call the restaurant. The waitress, who also is the owner, remembers us, then says, "Since you were good enough to call, I'll forget about the bill."

We mail her a check, tip included, when we return home. A cafe can't operate for long if stiffed by too many customers.

We label Utica a hidden jewel among Indiana's small town treasures.

The hill which rings Utica turns to a bluff up river where Upper River Road is lined for some distance with homes. A development called Longview Beach is on a dead end street. Expensive homes have double exposure, lawns in front reaching to the river, windows in back looking out toward steep bluffs.

Homes on the bluffs, which look across Longview Beach and the river to Kentucky, are more exclusive, gates blocking would-be sightseers.

HILLS AND HOLLOWS

And Economic Opportunity

River roads end at Longview Beach, so we drive up on the ridge toward Ind. 62, the George Rogers Clark Highway, which runs northeast into Charlestown. Developments have taken over farm land, houses growing where cattle once grazed.

The Indiana Army Ammunition Plant, closed by the government, is now for sale, most of its buildings abandoned. Huge signs proclaim, "5 Miles of Economic Opportunities" and "20 Miles of Perimeter Fence." The land stretches to the Ohio to the east.

Past Charlestown, we take Bull Creek Road, which follows Bull Creek, toward the river. Signs warn of a winding, steep hill. It is wise to heed the warning. The road drops into a developing resort area; some mobile homes are already in place along the river. "Building sites 100 feet wide," are advertised.

Blue Ridge Road leads up river, winding past a cattle farm before rising over a steep elevation to a farm appropriately named "River Echo." Somehow we find ourselves on Orchard Road where homes are few, traffic is light and "No Trespassing" signs are numerous. An outdated map of Clark County is our only guide. What little sense of direction we have leads to the Charlestown-Bethlehem Road.

Suddenly the road descends a steep hill, the lanes barely protected by guard rails as they dip toward Little Creek. Bags of trash, dumped by polluters, litter the banks above a deep valley, which appears more like a setting in eastern Kentucky or West Virginia than in Indiana.

We wind our way down another decline into Ohio River bottomland where farms are bigger, more productive. At last the familiar town of Bethlehem is in sight.

BETHLEHEM

A Family Business

Bethlehem remains much as it has for decades. The store is gone, the nearest one now eight miles west at New Washington.

No big developments, no subdivisions are planned to change the character of the town that looks like it belongs in another place and another time.

Oh, one of the old brick homes is now a bed and breakfast and its nearby barn converted to the Inn of Bethlehem. But there are no other businesses except Tom Brewer's antiques and furniture repair shop.

The post office. Zip Code 47104, remains in its little 8 by 10 feet building where it moved when the general store closed. Dorothy Selmier is postmaster, but her niece, Lora Eickholtz, is filling in for her on this day. "Not much happening here that I know of," Lora says. She helped put the Bethlehem postmark on cards last Christmas. "It seemed like we had more mail than usual," she recalls.

The post office is a family affair. "When my mom was postmaster here she hired Dorothy to be her assistant. When Mom moved over to Otisco, Aunt Dorothy became postmaster here."

The Bethlehem School is now marked as "historic property" and is being preserved by the Bethlehem Township Heritage Preservation Association with some funding help from the Historic Landmarks Foundation of Indiana.

The school grounds are used for the annual Autumn on the River Festival the third weekend of October. Old, new, and former residents cooperate in that endeavor which features dulcimer music, craft booths and tours of town in horse-drawn trains.

There is little new development around the community. Some towns are better left unchanged. Bethlehem may be one of them.

No roads lead up river. We drive over the ridge and depart Clark for Jefferson County.

JEFFERSON COUNTY

Established 1810 and named for Thomas Jefferson, the author of the Declaration of Independence and third president. Population 30,000. Area mainly hilly with farms in the valleys and on the high ground to the north.

MARBLE HILL
An Idea That Failed

No roads lead near the river as it winds its way onto a plateau in southern Jefferson County. A sign, unusual in rural areas, pleads with motorists to "Protect Our Children."

Ahead is a failed dream, a hulking, rusty reminder of an idea that failed. It is the remains of what was to have been the Marble Hill nuclear power plant. As cost overruns and unforeseen expenses ran into the billions, Public Service Indiana (now PSI Energy) stopped construction, leaving a monument to a good idea gone sour.

Rail spurs to the cooling towers remain unused. Giant upright skeletons remain, their steel arms holding no electric transmission lines.

At nearby Paynesville, small and unincorporated, a man stops working in his tool shed to give us directions on how to reach Hanover.

SALUDA

Graduates Remembered

Saluda High School closed years ago, but its alumni are not forgotten. The names of every graduate of the school, from 1910 through 1960, are etched on a limestone marker on the school ground. The bell from the school hangs over the monument.

Students, once the Lions, now attend Southwestern High at Hanover and root for the Rebels.

It is a Saturday, trash pickup day, and families are bringing filled plastic bags by the pickup load to a huge dumpster parked on the school grounds.

HANOVER

Awesome Power

South of Hanover, County Road 500 South leads to another vista onto the Ohio at a hairpin turn. The route at river's edge to the north is closed so we return to the ridge and pass neat rolling farms, two of which are big dairy operations, one a beef cattle business.

The road passes Southwestern Elementary and High Schools on its way into the old section of Hanover which remains almost as it has for decades, the newer developments out on Ind. 62.

Hanover College, which has perhaps Indiana's most beautiful campus, sits on an elevation, a circular road around the bluff opening a panoramic view of the river below. It is a photographer's delight, the only unsightliness the giant smokestacks of the generating station below.

Together, the power plants and the view illustrate the importance of the river. It is a source of power, a means of transportation and an attraction to tourists.

MADISON
Buried Treasures

Ind. 56 leaves Ind. 62 north of Hanover and winds down the bluff past the power plant toward Madison. Off to the north is the south entrance to Clifty Falls State Park another of Indiana's recreational jewels. The park, too, offers another vista of the river below. Its inn has affordable rooms, its restaurant good food at reasonable prices.

Hiking trails in the park lead to waterfalls and through deep-bouldered canyons.

Unlike many river towns, Madison has maintained its original business district and most of the buildings on Main Street are occupied and in good condition. Some like the Steinhardt-Hansen store are worth visiting.

Many of the homes are street front houses, leaving the area near the river much as it has been for years.

On a street near the river, Bob Mann is removing paint from bricks on an ancient house during off hours from his job at a steel mill over in Kentucky.

"I think it (the house) dates back to before the 1860s, somewhere around that time," he said. "I excavated a couple of privy pits out in the back and found some wine bottles that were dated before the Civil War."

He laughs. "That's a taboo subject for some people around here (determining dates by the remains of outhouses), but the treasures are in the privies," he adds. "I found items like feathered-edge plates that were broken and thrown away, booze bottles, old pipes used by smokers."

He obviously has learned the lifestyles of earlier residents. "Husbands sometimes went out to the privies to do their smoking and drinking if they weren't allowed to do those things inside. So that's where the contraband went. Down in the toilet pits.

"When the pits filled up, the owners topped them off with ashes, then covered them with clay," he explains.

Restoration of old homes is a slow process. He bought his place about six years ago, made it his home and continues his work to restore it. "Eventually I'll get the bricks all tucked up and a new roof on it. This is my baby," he confesses.

"You all be careful," he says, treating a stranger as a friend, as we drive away.

His dedication is not to be doubted. Mann, in a quiet way, is doing his part to make Madison a better place. So are other residents, contributing funds for the Madison Riverfront Project which is restoring the park along the Ohio.

Donors are advised to "buy a brick, $30." The more affluent can purchase benches for $500, columns for $2,000 or lights for $3,000. All contributors — individuals, organizations, businesses — are identified.

Those gifts are why the six block area is called the Madison Riverfront Walk of Pride. "Donations shape its future," a sign reads. There is work yet to be done and more donors are sought.

Facing the river on a two-block lot is the Lanier Mansion, tastefully landscaped with flowers and blooming plants. Tours of the house, now a state historic site, are permitted and walkers and bikers are free to use the grounds.

It was James F. D. Lanier who loaned the state $400,000 during the Civil War to equip troops. He later arranged additional funding for loans to save the credit of the state.

A leisurely walking trip through Madison is recommended for there is much to see, old churches, old buildings, too numerous to mention as tourism promoters say.

* * *

Ind. 56 follows the Ohio upstream, river banks at times lined with mobile homes anchored in place, some for weekend retreats, a few as permanent residences.

We are on what is called the Ohio River Scenic Route, a road that will hug the river for much of its 53 twisting miles to Aurora.

Guard rails protect drivers from the river where two barges meet, one headed up river, the other down. A few miles ahead, a third barge is on its way downstream, once again accentuating the Ohio's importance to commerce.

BROOKSBURG

A Man Called "Bill"

A store with no name out front, only a small "groceries and meat" sign, is open. Inside, Charles "Bill" Adams asks about the weather outside as he rubs a two-day stubble of whiskers.

Adams is overseeing the store for his mother, who is 88. "She has been here (at the store) 47 years. We used to do a pretty good business, but we don't do much any more," he explains.

"She (his mother) ought to be out of here, but I can't get her to leave. She can't watch the store and I don't wanta do it. I retired once. Did a little bit of everything," he says, making it clear he isn't too interested in doing anything to add to that "everything."

It's the only retail outlet in town, though, and the men in the back wouldn't have a place to talk if someone wasn't around to keep the store open.

Brooksburg no longer has a post office. "We let it get away," Bill says, explaining, "we didn't know they were going to close it, until it . was too late."

The town wasn't always this quiet. "I think there was a girls' college in a stone house I owned, but I don't know the years. We once had a grade school (through 8 grades) which I attended. Then I went to Madison to high school."

In its earlier days, back before cars replaced river traffic, Brooksburg had five or six taverns, a sawmill, barber shop, "stuff like that," Adams adds. "I remember when they would bring cattle, hogs and merchandise to the landing up on the river. If you ordered anything of any size, that's where it came from. The river."

It is another community that was devastated by the 1937 flood. "The water was up on that door there," Adams says, pointing to the entrance. "The town never grew much after that. It never had much room to grow, anyhow, the river being on one side, the crick (Indian-Kentuck Creek) on one side and hills to the north."

The store now is the town's gathering spot, as well as a place to buy a few things which may save a resident a drive into Madison. "We usually have people in here. We don't sell coffee, but they come in and talk. Everybody knows everybody in a small town, you know."

Adams pauses, laughs again. "Oh, I didn't mention that the women burned half the taverns down. They just don't understand men."

It is obvious Bill Adams makes a good host for the men who gather at the back of the little store.

* * *

Up river, the road continues to wind, staying within sight of the river. A few marinas are on the river beyond some flat farm fields. A farmhouse, its bricks painted white, is still occupied as it has been since the days when America was new and Indiana was not yet a state.

The community of Lamb and Switzerland County are around the next bend in the road.

SWITZERLAND COUNTY

Established 1814 and named after the European country from which the first settlers came. Sometimes called "The Rhineland of America." Population 7,800. County seat is at Vevay, the county's major commercial center.

LAMB

A Taxing Day

Len and Carol Woelfle have a window to the world from their shop/home at a wide spot on Ind. 56 called Lamb. Traffic is to their front, the river a short distance to the south. They own The Halfway House — "prints, frames, custom framing, gifts, collectibles, country furniture," the sign out front reads.

Mrs. Woelfle invites us in, offers coffee, invites us to look around.

The Woelfles moved here from the west side of Cincinnati and both agree Lamb is a far different place, "completely."

"People down here are so much friendlier. You know all your neighbors, even if they are 10 miles away. In Cincinnati, you sometimes don't know the people who live across the street," Mrs. Woelfle asserts.

They live in the part of the house not used as show rooms for their items. Another building is being added for the crafts they sell.

"Would you all like a cup of coffee?" Len also asks, coming in to the show room in sock feet, a friendly greeting written on his face.

"We've been trying to make a living, but it doesn't look like we're doing too good," he explains. It is tax deadline day and he is referring to the return he has spread out on a table in the kitchen. "We owe," he moans, then adds, "Thank God for credit cards."

"Trying to make a living and paying taxes is something else," Len Woelfle moans. "You'd think with everything we got around here we would be making a fortune. But you take out what we've got in it, we don't have much left."

He repeats an invitation: "You are always welcome to come in for a cup of coffee."

The shop is open from 9 a.m. to 9 p.m. Despite long hours in a taxing business, the Woelfles have retained their friendliness.

VEVAY

Strolling Through Town

The road ahead to Vevay (pronounced Vee-Vee) is dotted with tobacco barns, old houses made of native stone, camp grounds and house trailers on the river banks.

Ind. 129 drops over the bluffs to meet Ind. 56 at the west edge of Vevay, not far from the Ogle House, a lodge-type motel where the restaurant specializes in German food.

There is much to see in Vevay and residents like Prestine Chapman are delighted to tell visitors places to visit. She is executive director of the Switzerland County Convention and Visitor's Bureau, one of the best tourist bureaus in the state, we have found. She is promoter of the town and Switzerland County, always eager to aid visitors who stop at her office.

Most of Vevay can be seen on a leisurely walk. Its historic homes are marked with dates and names; for example, "the Roxy House, 1814, home of Aunt Lucy Detraz, fifth white child born in the county."

The Armstrong Tavern is said to be the oldest known building in Indiana used as a Masonic meeting place. Erected in 1816 as an inn, it became a home for the lodge in 1819.

It is just one of the ancient structures that can be seen on a leisurely walk along Market Street from Arch Street to Ferry Street, then north a block to Main Street past the Switzerland County Courthouse. Another area to view the homes, enjoy history, and recall an earlier time is bounded by Ferry, Main, Turnpike and Pike Streets.

Still standing on Main Street is the home of Edward Eggleston, the author of *The Hoosier Schoolmaster.*

At Vevay's main intersection a town worker, equipped with a push cart, broom and shovel, scoops up debris. Cleanliness is part of the heritage of this Swiss community.

In the business district, Danner's Hardware is in operation as it has been for decades, said to be the oldest continuous business in the state operated in the same location.

"Bear" Bladen, considered by some as one of Vevay's favorite personalities, is not at the Indiana Puzzle Antique Mall as he usually is. His wife, Martha is, working at the business while on spring vacation from her classroom at Harrison, Ohio.

The Bladens dog "Tootie," a bandana around its neck, greets visitors at the door. The mall has two floors of items, tastefully placed with room between the aisle for viewing.

"Bear," known in Vevay as a fascinating story teller, is "a writer whose fascinating works enthrall all ages," a tourism flyer boasts. He is noted for his stories about life in Patriot, another Switzerland County community where he grew up.

News is mostly good in Vevay. It's the kind of town where the local paper, *The Reveille-Enterprise*, puts positive stories such as "Switzerland County High School Honor Society Inducts Members" and "High School Band Places Fifth In Washington Parade" on Page One.

Other towns should be as fortunate.

MARKLAND

Comings and Goings

Ind. 56 goes north from Vevay through the heart of Switzerland County, but Ind. 156 starts in town and continues along the river.

It leads to the town of Markland, where little remains. The general store is closed, so is a garage. There is no post office. The town does generate some news, though, the comings and goings of . residents reported by correspondent Vandora Bennett in her column in the county seat newspaper.

Upstream are the Markland Dam and Locks, which can be seen by crossing the Ohio on Ind. 101 to the Kentucky side of the river.

FLORENCE

Forget The Hassle

Another PSI Energy generating plant is up river from Markland past fields that edge close to Ind. 156.

Turtle Creek Harbor, a good spot for river sportsmen, is at the mouth of Turtle Creek where it flows into the Ohio. Luxury boats are anchored at the marina.

In Florence, postmaster Floyd Canada, who has been on the job 14 years, talks about the town. "It's just a small settlement with a lot of old people. At one time there were six groceries, a shoe cobbler shop, a bank and three restaurants. Now there is nothing but a grocery store, the post office and a church."

The residents, though, are friendly. "Common folks, kind people," he adds, showing his appreciation for his customers.

Despite efforts to bring riverboat gambling to Switzerland County, Canada surmises, "I don't think a majority of the people here want it. They don't want to live life in the fast lanes or have that kind of stuff here. They are older and laid back and they don't want all the excitement and hassle riverboats would bring."

Canada is soft-spoken, friendly and doesn't use swear words, even though he says he wasn't aware, until told, that Florence once had an Anti-Swearing Society, which fined its 75 members for uttering profanities.

PATRIOT

Unappreciated Beauty

Ind. 156 remains close to the river, following its course as it turns from east to north. Just off the road and surrounded by fields is the Concord Community Church, organized 1884. "Come celebrate God's love with us," a sign reads.

Pickup trucks are more common than cars on the road which rises and falls with the terrain. Good views of the river are numerous.

Patriot was a much larger community before much of it was destroyed by the 1937 flood. It never recovered despite its long history as a river town.

At the Town Hall, clerk-treasurer Pam Hutchinson tells us about the Patriot of today: "The population is 191, a figure that has gone down over the years. We have a lot of elderly people and we all, regardless of age, like our little town.

"Some people, though, may not appreciate it (the natural beauty of the area) as much as visitors who spend weekends and vacations in and around Patriot," she adds.

It's a common complaint. Folks sometimes don't always recognize the beauty that surrounds them.

A three member town council and Mrs. Hutchinson administer the water and sewer utilities.

It is donations month for the Volunteer Fire Department, which depends on contributions and revenue from bingo games conducted in the Town Hall.

Patriot has a grocery, service station, post office, two churches and pages of history. A stone jail, 12 feet by 12 feet, still stands as it has since 1820 not far from a cemetery that is even older.

Riverboat gambling seems inevitable for the Ohio. Mrs. Hutchinson is not one of those who wants it. "I don't like the idea myself. The county needs the money, but there are other ways we can get it. I think it would do more harm than good."

* * *

The Patriot Yacht Club is up river from Patriot along Ind. 156 from which motorists can see across the river to Kentucky and the cabins that are on the banks of the Ohio. Some nice farms are ahead. So is an expansive aggregates business, it being politically incorrect to say "gravel pit" in these days of precise descriptions.

Two barges meet at a bend in the Ohio which turns slightly west around a bend. The road is so close to the river its banks have been shored up to keep them from eroding into the river.

The Ohio makes a sweeping turn back to the east and the road follows.

OHIO COUNTY

Indiana's smallest county, in size and population (5,350). One of younger counties, being established in 1844. Named for the river that forms its entire eastern border. Rising Sun is county seat and only town of size.

We enter Ohio County at a place called North Landing, a wide spot on Ind. 156. Up ahead the river is lined with residences.

We see our first semi since leaving Madison, a True-Value truck delivering merchandise to what few hardware stores there are along the river.

Ind. 56 has finished winding its way through the high ground and returns to the river north of the Switzerland County line. Ind. 156 ends and Ind. 56 again joins the "Scenic Route."

Two miles down river from Rising Sun, the river bank is lined with mobile homes anchored in place amid conventional homes. Traffic has increased because we are nearing Cincinnati and the afternoon commute is beginning.

RISING SUN

Volunteerism

Lois Mora is finding volunteerism can be a full-time effort. She is at work in an office in a river front hotel, the Empire House, circa 1812, that is now the home of the Rising Sun/Ohio County Tourism Bureau.

"This your day to work?" we ask.

She laughs. "It's my day to work every day. I took early retirement and volunteered when someone said I wouldn't have to work much. But I seem to be here full time. I'd never done a brochure before," she explains, holding a 1995 visitor's guide which includes a calendar of Rising Sun events.

It's an informative pamphlet, one as informative as could be made by a professional.

The tourism bureau is new, still in its organizational stage. "It is all volunteer now, but we hope to be able to raise funds for a paid director," Mrs. Mora explains.

The bureau may not be able to find anyone as community minded as she is. "Why should tourists come to this area?" we ask. She does not hesitate to reply:

"Oh it's wonderful. No. 1, we have the scenic route (Ind. 56 and Ind. 156 from Madison to Aurora). We are trying to get national recognition for that road and I am on a committee for that.

"No. 2, we have the friendliest people, I think, anywhere. We are the smallest county and one of the smallest cities (population 2,325) in Indiana," she stops counting but continues to enumerate the good things the county offers:

"We have the river, of course, which is one of the most attractive features and one that offers a lot of activities. We have antique shops. It is just a very nice place to visit for a day or to stay over at the bed and breakfast homes.

"The quality of living is just phenomenal. It is a completely different way of life (than in cities where she has lived), laid back, peaceful, quiet. I've never met people who are so concerned about their neighbors and their community. It is just a totally different way of life," she stresses, citing the major cities where she has lived.

"To me it is the greatest place in the world," she adds, speaking with all the conviction of a professional tourism director.

Next door to the hotel is the original Rising Sun post office, believed to have been built in 1816, its logs now hidden by siding.

Whitlock Memorial Overlook is on the river. It was the Whitlock family that built fine furniture and operated a lumberyard and fireworks factory. And it was J. W. "Row" Whitlock who designed and raced the Hoosier, a famed racing boat of the 1920s.

On a rise above any threat of flooding is the Ohio County Courthouse, the state's oldest seat of government which has been in continuous use since 1845. Four pillars accentuate the Greek Revival structure, small but apparently large enough for the state's smallest county.

"Jack's Place, Family Dining," the menu says, but it also is a hangout for men who like to swap stories and comment on the news of the day. A sign on the wall reads:

1 Coffee -12 refills.......$.60.

1 hour same chair........$.85.

Half-morning with one table move.....$1.25.

All morning, 1 restroom visit.............$1.75.

All day, bring lunch.................$3.50.

Spoon Wavers   Liars

Thumb Snappers   Fanny Pinchers

Whistlers   Cup Wavers

All pay double

Every town needs a place where loafers are welcome.

The city's business district extends almost to the river on Main Street past stores, the newspaper office, antique shops and a pharmacy. A liquor store is appropriately named "River Spirits." The brick Presbyterian Church built in 1832 is for sale.

(A few weeks later, Rising Sun won its effort to be the site of a riverboat casino. It may bring new jobs, new visitors, new hotels. Somehow, though, the Rising Sun of today seems too good to change, but that is a decision for those who live here to make).

* * *

Ind. 56 no longer runs through the community of French, bypassing it nearer the river. A number of homes remain but the only businesses are out on the new road. To the north is Laughery Creek which separates Ohio and Dearborn Counties.

DEARBORN COUNTY

Established 1803 as Indiana's third county. Named for Gen. Henry Dearborn, secretary of war under Thomas Jefferson. Population 40,000 and growing as families move from Cincinnati area. Bordered on the south by the Ohio River, the east by Ohio, the state.

Laughery Creek has played an important part in the area's history. It was August 24, 1781, at the mouth of the creek at the Ohio that 100 Indians surprised and defeated Col. Archibald Lochry and 107 Pennsylvania volunteers. Lochry's men were en route to join George Rogers Clark in a campaign against Fort Detroit. The creek is a memorial to Lochry, but his name was misspelled and no correction was ever made.

AURORA
View From The Top

On Aurora's south side, men and women sit on benches at a small park and watch the peaceful river make its gentle sweep around the bend.

A historical marker notes Jesse L. Holman's role in the development of the town. Judge Holman was an early statesman, preacher, educator and federal justice.

Overlooking the city from its imposing hillside location is Hillforest, a home placed on the National Register of Historic Places in 1972. Its steamboat-like appearance is created by rounded central colonnades topped by a "pilot house" belvedere. Hillforest was home to Thomas Gaff, a prominent river shipper, from 1856 to 1884.

The home was acquired by the Hillforest Historical Foundation and is open to visitors.

There are, however, even more imposing views of the Ohio Valley. We take Langley Heights Street up a steep incline to York Avenue. The peak provides a wondrous view of Aurora, which from this point looks like a New England settlement. The vista overlooks

View of Ohio River from above Aurora

three states, Indiana to the north, Ohio to the northeast and Kentucky to the east.

Aurora, current population about 3,900, was once a major trade center, a past still reflected in two streets, one named Importing, the other Exporting. Barges still are loaded at the river.

Much of the city's downtown remains, including the Steamboat Clinton Restaurant, which offers "River Town dining."

Ind. 56 and the Ohio Scenic Route end at U.S. 50 which leads up the river to Lawrenceburg and eventually to Cincinnati. U.S. 50 between Aurora and Lawrenceburg, rival river cities, is lined with fast food restaurants and businesses.

LAWRENCEBURG
Whiskey City

The giant Seagrams distillery almost dominates the Lawrenceburg skyline as it has since 1857. A sign — "Lawrenceburg —
Home of Seagrams — Spirit of Quality" — greets visitors.

It is no mystery why the state's fourth oldest city is often called
"Whiskey City."

It seems appropriate that one of the better dining spots in the
area is Whisky's Restaurant at U.S. 50 and Front Street. It boasts
that "the best ribs in Cincinnati are in Lawrenceburg." Not many
diners argue otherwise.

Chances are Samuel C. Vance never visualized a "Whiskey
City" would rise in the place he named for his wife, Mary Morris
Lawrence, in 1802. The Federal style mansion Vance built in 1818
still stands, but in less elegant surroundings than those early days
when guests arrived by riverboat and reached the mansion through
an avenue of cedar trees.

Vance is said to have been a friend of William Henry Harrison,
who would later become president.

The Jesse Hunt house — once the King Hotel — is in old
Lawrenceburg down by the levee. Legend has it that another president, Andrew Johnson, was among its guests. A number of other
homes of that period remain.

If a county can have a one-stop government center, Dearborn
County has it. The Courthouse, other offices, the Law Enforcement
Center and the county library are conveniently located in a complex
in the downtown area.

It is the first courthouse we have seen on this tour that has
guards and metal detectors at its doors, evidence that even small-
city Hoosiers are becoming concerned about violence.

The limestone courthouse fronted with four columns was built
in 1871, but the other buildings are newer.

A CSX train passes on the tracks near the courthouse, breaking the stillness of the day for it is a quiet afternoon in Lawrenceburg. The brick depot still stands, but is no longer a stopping point
for the railroad which owns the tracks.

Lawrenceburg, population 4,400, is the only community in Dearborn County that has kept its high school. South Dearborn is an incorporation of Aurora, Dillsboro and Moores Hill; East Central a merger of Bright, Guilford and Sunman.

* * *

I-275, the bypass that links Ohio, Indiana and Kentucky, cuts across the northeast edge of Lawrenceburg. It is there that the Ohio River no longer forms the southern boundary of Indiana. The eastern border, a direct line stretching north begins its division of Indiana and Ohio for 135 miles.

Oberting Road leads north out of Lawrenceburg to State Line Road where a sign on a concrete post marks the state line boundary that was established October 11, 1798.

To the northwest a development of luxury homes rises on the hills overlooking the valley to the east.

It has been the hills, up to 700 feet above sea level, the expansive scenery and the peaceful setting that has led dozens of families to move from the Cincinnati area. The lots are affordable, the view, almost mountain-like, exceptional. It is a far different place than expensive city lots with restricted space.

Up the road, a new golf course and another new housing development is under construction.

BRIGHT

As in Future

We head northeast in search of the old community of Bright, a small town now surrounded by the fifth fastest growing suburban area in the state.

"Future home of the Bright Senior Citizen's Center" a sign reads. It is, however, younger people who now are occupying the area, changing the landscape, crowding the schools.

A sign at the Trading Post, a store and restaurant, informs residents of Miller Township to call the Archdiocese of Indianapolis if they are interested in starting a Catholic church and school.

Not far away a new public elementary school is under construction.

New retail businesses are moving into the area, following the rapid gains in population. The Bright community which includes parts of Harrison, Logan and Miller Townships has a population of about 6,000, increasing by almost 65 percent in the last decade.

East Central, the high school that serves the area, has had rapid enrollment gains, from 993 to 1,216 from 1988 to 1995.

Few of the newer residents likely are aware that Bright once was known as Saltillo because of its salt springs. It was later called Bunkem after a resident said Saltillo was a bunkem of a name. It was here in 1886 that Knowles Shaw, who preached at a church in Bright, wrote the words to "Bringing in the Sheaves."

That is history, however. Bright has outgrown its past and chances are its newer residents are too busy looking ahead to look back.

* * *

We take Jameson Road northeast from Bright, through more wooded hills. The few modest older houses are dwarfed by new huge structures. The road drops sharply as it winds into the Whitewater River valley.

An occasional motorist ignores the turns in the road to pass slower cars, the pace of the area accelerating as more people occupy the hills.

A road follows the Whitewater upstream through bottomland near the Ohio border. The development has ended and farms remain as they have for decades.

We want to make sure we are on a road to somewhere. A man with Ohio license plates on his pickup has stopped to open a gate. He points the way north for he is not eager to talk. His new neighbors may change his disposition, teach him Hoosier hospitality.

WEST HARRISON
Lost In Time

West Harrison's past seems bigger than its present. It played a big part in the development of northeastern Dearborn County. Its two hotels were stopping points as settlers moved into the state around 1820.

Two decades or so later, the Whitewater Canal opened, bringing mills, distilleries and shops. When the canal failed, the Whitewater Valley Railway kept West Harrison open to commerce.

Today, West Harrison appears lost and isolated in the shadow of I-74 as it carries traffic to Cincinnati.

Two interchanges are nearby however, one at Harrison, West Harrison's neighbor to the east, one northeast at U.S. 52.

* * *

A county road runs under the interstate and winds its way through the rugged terrain two miles north into Franklin County.

On the East

FRANKLIN COUNTY

Established 1811, five years before statehood, as Indiana's seventh county and named for Ben Franklin. Considered state's cradle of civilization because many pioneers entered the area through the Whitewater Valley. Population 20,000. Hilly in the south, level with some good farm lands along the border to the north.

ROCKDALE

Hoosier Country

The land remains hilly just north of the Dearborn-Franklin County border in this area around the community of Rockdale.

A barking dog and the roar of the unnamed creek break the morning silence in the tiny town. The stream is higher than normal, its current more rapid after a heavy rain.

Britt Harry joins us at the roadside, confirming, "This is the big town of Rockdale. I've lived here 20 years and it has never been much bigger than it is now," he explains, looking north to a half dozen homes built between the county road and the creek.

"What do people do here for a living?" he repeats, then adds, "Not much." It is early morning and he's a young man not given to a lot of talk when the sun is still low to the east.

"Do people down here think of themselves as Hoosiers or Buckeyes?" we ask.

"Hoosiers," he replies, proudly, emphatically even though Ohio is just a stone-from-the-creek throw.

The only gathering spot appears to be the Rockdale Methodist Church. There are no businesses, but there is enough traffic, however, for "Children at Play" warnings.

* * *

A hill rises from the valley and Drewersburg Road runs past a big-scale farm operation to where the land is level. Drewersburg isn't any bigger than Rockdale, but it does have a fire department where signs call attention to its fund-raising "whole hog sausage breakfast."

Small communities don't always ask for more tax money. Sometimes they raise their own funds as Drewersburg's fire department is doing.

* * *

East of Drewersburg, a development marked "North Fork Executive Sites" lures Ohioans in search of big lots on rolling building sites.

Chuckholes on the state line road provide equal opportunity repavement to both Indiana and Ohio.

It is an area of contrasts. A farm is abandoned, its house empty, its gates closed, its mail box rusted, all hints of absentee ownership. Not far away a silo stands forlorn, its barn gone. The farm house is being razed, board by board.

Within a short distance farm homes are well maintained, lawns green, outbuildings painted.

The land improves as we drive north through the eastern part of the county. The hills to the southeast fade in the distance.

The road extends to Ind. 252 which leads east to a place called Scipio. A narrow bridge over a small stream at a turn of the road divides Indiana from Ohio. Scipio's six houses are split, three in Indiana, three in Ohio.

A "Morgan General Store" sign is on one building. So is "Casey's Grocery." It is obvious the place hasn't been open under any name for years.

An "Indiana Welcomes You" sign greets motorists from the east, although this is not a main doorway into Indiana.

BROOKVILLE

Too Good To Miss

It is six miles from the border, but Brookville has too much to offer tourists to miss.

It was here at the junction of the east and west forks of the Whitewater River that the Whitewater Canal was started in 1836. And this was the gateway to Indiana for many immigrants, mainly Germans who made their way into the midwest through Cincinnati in the 1830s.

Homes with historical significance are numerous. The Hermitage, for example, has 17 rooms with a 100-foot long porch. One of the older buildings is the former First Methodist Church built in 1822, and still used as a Baptist Church. Historical markers are numerous.

The business area remains much as it has for decades in the county seat of 2,550 residents. It is a town too few see and too many miss now that I-74 has replaced U.S. 52 between Indianapolis and Cincinnati.

* * *

Ind. 252, a route that at times seems to follow a trail of a slithering snake, straightens as it rolls up and down over rolling terrain. At Mount Carmel the terrain flattens into good farm land.

MOUNT CARMEL

Bigger Not Better

Bob Hoffman and his wife run one of the few businesses in Mount Carmel, a small town three miles east of the Ohio border on Ind. 252. They operate the "Mount Carmel Country Store and Ice Cream Corner."

Hoffman moved to Indiana from Ohio after he started a 10-year career as an elementary teacher at Springfield Township School. Back then high school students were attending Whitewater which later became part of Brookville, then Franklin County High School.

Like many others, he questions the merits of huge school corporations compared with the township schools of mid-century, citing the loss of community identity, spirit and cohesiveness.

Chances are he might not be happy in a big school setting, preferring to remain part of Mount Carmel as a businessman rather than being an educator elsewhere.

"We try to keep a lot of things in the store which we've had since 1990," he explains "It's not a hugely successful business, but it makes a little money. We have a school bus route and I write health and life insurance."

As he says, the store has an assortment of items for sale, from hand-dipped ice cream to wearing apparel. A table allows customers to talk, sip coffee or soft drinks and remember the Mount Carmel of an earlier time.

Hoffman has heard their stories. "I guess probably 100 years ago this little town was even more thriving than it is now. At the turn of the century," they said, "the town had two grain mills and several stores. It was quite a thriving little community."

It still is a nice town surrounded by good farm land, made better by Bob Hoffman's decision to stay here after leaving the classroom.

THE BORDER

Two States United

We take a county road north, then east again to the state line in search of a border town called Peoria. The land is rolling, the farms larger on the plateau which offers a 360-degree vista of the pollution-free horizon, its skyline dotted with farm storage elevators.

We turn north off Merrill Road onto State Line Road to Peoria. The CSX railroad still cuts through what town there is. The elevator is closed, but its storage towers still stand.

Chances are Peoria was a bigger, busier place when farmers depended on trains to export their products and deliver supplies.

State Line Road continues north, the pavement smooth, traffic almost non-existent, the view into Indiana clear. Only the road markers indicate there is an Indiana or an Ohio, the states blending into harmony as the founders of the nation intended.

The road runs straight and true in sharp contrast to the serpentine Ohio River that forms the state's south boundary.

RAYMOND

And Mixerville

The paved State Line Road ends, but another route leads toward a spot called Raymond. A collapsing barn is in sharp contrast to a well-manicured farm home and painted outbuildings across the way.

The area rises above its surroundings and the view extends for cloud-free miles in all directions.

It is obvious Raymond is an agriculture community in the heart of Franklin County's rich farm land.

At Hofer's Inc. farm store, Larry Hofer, talks about Raymond: "It's a little farm town that never changes much. The land is good for several miles. Like one of our customers said, 'you get to the Whitewater River west and the terrain gets rougher and the ground poorer.' This is the best land in Franklin County. This is black loam. Over west of the river it is clay."

The Hofers are of German descent, but "a little of everything settled this area," Larry relates. He tells an interesting story about Mixerville, a town up the road:

"There weren't any trains in the early days in this area and farmers had to herd their stock to market. They'd drive their turkeys, which would get sore feet, to Mixerville where there was a tar pit. The turkeys would be run through the tar which would coat their feet for protection.

"The farmers stayed overnight in a hotel in Mixerville before renewing the turkey drive on toward Cincinnati."

He finishes the story, then asks, "Did you ever hear tell of that?" We confess we had not.

A train goes through town. "It's the only one of the day," Larry says. It no longer stops at Raymond. Farm products are now trucked in and out.

Larry confesses that Raymond hasn't changed much over the years. "No one has even built a new house here. Bet you don't run onto many places like that," he says.

We don't, but neither do we meet many men as friendly as Larry Hofer and his brother, Darrell.

Mixerville, a town with 40 or so houses, is a short distance northeast of Raymond. It is a few days after the federal building blast in Oklahoma City and a number of flags are at half staff.

An old two-story brick could have been the hotel where the turkey herders stayed, but there is no one here to ask. No tar pits remain, either.

* * *

North of Mixerville silos, Harvestores and metal granaries dominate the landscape along the state line. To the north is the town of New Bath, which surprisingly has a big bank operation.

NEW BATH
Less Stress

Tom Agee is a good man to ask about New Bath. He lives in Cincinnati and commutes daily to his job as town postmaster. It's a far different environment than he experienced when he was director of mail in Cincinnati.

When a reduction in personnel was ordered, supervisors were offered transfers to small post offices. Agee appears to have made the transition smoothly.

"It's nice out here. A lot less stressful. We have 36 boxes rented, and a rural route with 125 customers. It is a typical rural post office."

The post office is in New Bath, but the postmark is Bath, an older community to the west.

Chances are if it wasn't for the bank there would be no post office at all. The bank, which has more than 50 employees despite its remote location, does business in most states, mortgage loans its specialty, Agee explains.

"Other than that," he adds, "there isn't much to say about the town. The area is mostly farm land which is owned by five or six families. It once was a bigger community, but about the only things left besides the bank are the feed mill and stock yards. The store closed, then reopened and closed again."

Agee hasn't noticed much difference between Hoosiers and Buckeyes, now that he has worked in both Indiana and Ohio. "I've got relatives in both states. My mother is from down in Kentucky. Country people are country people. They are all pretty conservative and straight laced, I guess you could say."

Residents in New Bath would probably appreciate his appraisal.

* * *

New Bath is just a mile from Union County. We go east, then take a road near the border to the north.

UNION COUNTY

One of the state's smallest counties in size, about 12 miles wide, 14 miles deep. Only Ohio and Floyd are smaller. Population 7,000, only Ohio County having fewer residents. Established 1821 and named for the pursuit of common goals. Whitewater State Park is in the county.

———

Land remains good, farms prosperous, homes neat and orderly in southern Union County. Clothes whip from lines in the spring breeze.

A barn on a seldom traveled road is newly painted, "Red Man Tobacco — America's Best Chew," perhaps a rebirth of a somewhat forgotten form of advertisement.

COLLEGE CORNER
Friendly Coexistence

College Corner is a town that couldn't decide whether it wanted to be in Indiana or Ohio so it straddled the state line.

Even the grade school sits on the border, limestone blocks over each front door, the west engraved "Indiana," the east "Ohio."

Kindergarten through eighth grade students from both states attend the school, then move on to Union County (Ind.) High at Liberty.

The post office also is on the state line but it has an Ohio Zip Code. It is operating on Indiana time on this day, adding to the confusion.

A woman drops a letter off and comments. "It's crazy. I built a house about a mile out of town and have had to learn to deal with the situation."

So how do folks around here tell a Hoosier from a Buckeye?

The woman laughs. "I can tell a woman from a man, but I'm not sure I can tell a Hoosier from a Buckeye." She pauses, then adds on second thought, "Sometimes I'm not sure anymore about a man and a woman."

Hoosier or Buckeye, she has a sense of humor.

* * *

We drive north on State Line Road toward Ind. 44. We wave at a driver meeting us from the opposite direction. He does not return our greeting, our first snub since leaving Vincennes.

At Ind. 44, we turn west and drive through the farm country into Liberty the county seat, population 2,100.

LIBERTY

Generally Speaking

It is noon on a Friday, but there is little activity around the Union County square. Parking is available at the courthouse, a 100-year-old three-story limestone structure that dominates the business district.

A log cabin rebuilt at the southeast corner of Courthouse Square dates back to 1804 and is believed to be the oldest existing log structure in the county. It is a memorial to John Templeton, a Union County pioneer.

Liberty is an old town. Brick buildings from an earlier time line part of the square's east side. Churches date back to the mid-1800s. A large brick house, circa 1840, once was the Union County Seminary.

Markers note that Liberty was the home of Maj. Gen. Ambrose Burnsides, who for a time commanded the Union Army in the Civil War.

The town is in sharp contrast to the new Union County High School being built on the east side.

* * *

A paved road east of town on Ind. 44 passes the Union County poor farm, a reminder of the day before Social Security when counties housed the aging poor.

Cattle graze on rolling pastures, greened by spring rains.

At Hanna's Creek Christian Church, the bulletin board advises: "Pray Always. If Needed, Use Words." It is another of the religious messages we are recording on this trip.

KITCHEL

No Cowboy Shows

The land where Indians once roamed and Cowboys once played is quiet today.

The Indians left when the white man came. School consolidation brought an end to the Cowboys, which was the term for Kitchel High School athletic teams.

Part of the school still stands, unused. Playground equipment and the ball diamond remain, rusting tombstones in the cemetery of memories. Sounds of laughter among the Harrison Township students no longer echo across the town.

Like other towns, Kitchel lost its identity and much of its spirit when the school became part of Union County High and Cowboys became Patriots.

There is little activity in town, no businesses, no post office. What appears to have been a farm store is closed despite the vast farm fields that surround Kitchel.

WITTS STATION
Untrained Melody

The CSX tracks run north from Kitchel to Witts Station, two miles away. Witts Station, as hundreds of other towns, grew up with the railroad, then withered when trains became less important to the survival of agriculture.

No stop signs the mark train crossing. Perhaps motorists in the area know when the one train a day runs. The train station is gone and only a grain storage tower near the tracks stands as a testimony to a busier time.

What few houses that remain are well maintained. A town doesn't need to lose its pride when its importance wanes.

* * *

Farms spread east toward the state line, silos reaching toward the clear sky as Ind. 227 slices across the northeast corner of the county. Only a few wooded areas block the view, the horizon appearing endless to the north into Wayne County.

WAYNE COUNTY

Founded in 1810 and named for Gen. Anthony Wayne, a Revolutionary War hero noted for his victories over the Indians. Population 72,000, including 38,000 who live in Richmond.

BOSTON
A Storied Town

Ind. 227 enters the town of Boston in the southeast corner of Wayne County and meets old Ind. 122 at the main intersection.

It is spring, but some residents already are talking about the annual town-wide yard sale in the fall. Pat Stack, who lives in town, explains, "Most of the homes here set out what they'd like to sell, a house-to-house yard sale, normally held in late September or early October.

"What is nice about the sale is that Boston is an old community. Every year the older people put a few more of their collectibles out for sale so there are a lot of treasures to be found."

Enough he says to attract up to 1,500 shoppers, many of whom arrive with the sun.

Stack is visiting with the manager of the Auction House on the corner of Boston's main intersection. The manager will take part in the annual fall sale, but now he is preparing for his weekly auction which is just hours away.

"We start at 6 p.m. each Friday," the manager says, identifying himself only as "Weatherly," his last name, as men often do. "And I go as long as people are buying. When they quit, I quit. Some nights I knock it off at 9 p.m. Some nights I keep truckin' until 10:30 or 11, depending on how long they want to bid. Bidders come from everywhere, from over in Ohio and from Indiana towns within 40 or 50 miles."

It's Stack's turn to talk again, because he lives in Boston, has since he was born in 1952.

"The old timers have a lot of stories about all the things that were supposed to have happened here. Famous gangsters were said to have eaten at the restaurant here, but I don't know that for a fact. And there was talk about public hangings from that big oak in front of the fire station. I don't know if that is true, either."

It makes for good conversation, though. So does Stack's memories of the year Boston High School was forced to consolidate with Richmond in the 1960s. The town lost its athletic teams, the Terriers and both the town and its students lost their identities.

"Us farm kids had to go to school with Richmond city rats from then on. It hurt all of us, as well as the town."

The auction operator, laughs. "Hey, I was a Richmond city rat." Stack is not deterred:

"The school here closed in 1966 and I started to Richmond as a sophomore that fall before transportation was provided. The dean of boys told me, 'I don't really care how you Boston kids get to school.' So I had to hitchhike. The other Boston kids had to find their own ways, too."

He's still resentful. "Richmond didn't give a damn how we got to school since there really weren't a handful of us anyhow."

He pauses, then laughs again. "If Boston had remained open, the 1969 class might have had five, six graduates, depending on whether it was time to put the crops out or not. There were 600 some in the senior class at Richmond. The entire community of Boston didn't have that many people."

Boston still has its post office, but its restaurant is now a pool room. A few other businesses remain. So do churches, one of which promotes Sunday's sermon: "Reality Maps and Rolling Stones." It sounds interesting, but Sunday is two days away, and it's doubtful we would see any famous outlaws or public hangings in the interim.

* * *

North of Boston, the road makes a slight turn into Ohio to avoid a cemetery that straddles the state line on a ridge above a small creek.

The soil remains rich, the farms large, the vista expansive. South of Richmond, however, the terrain changes, becoming rolling as it reaches a suburban subdivision. A new development of large, expensive homes fronts on Green Mount Road which is lined with redbud trees, alive in their spring color.

RICHMOND

City of Roses

We drive into Richmond to U.S. 40, the old National Road, then turn west toward downtown past city parks and the Hayes Regional Arboretum, a 355-acre nature center.

This is the "City of Roses," but it is too early for rose gardens to be in bloom.

Although it is a Friday afternoon, few shoppers, no more than 50, are at the downtown mall, an open five-block park-like setting with brick walks.

By coincidence, 300 residents had attended a meeting the previous night to brainstorm about the future of downtown Richmond. Ideas about how to bring new life to the area were discussed with consultants, who were asked to present an action agenda later.

One of Richmond's worst tragedies is marked at the mall, a memorial to 41 persons who lost their lives in a tragic explosion of powder at a gun store April 6, 1966.

It is at the mall that we observe the first nasty encounter on this tour of Borderline Indiana. An elderly clerk hands a shopper three packs of cigarettes. They are not what the shopper wants so she tosses them in a waste basket and glowers threateningly at the clerk:

"Are you trying to get smart with me?" she asks, startling the clerk and customers waiting in line.

The clerk, who appears to be in her 70s, graciously gives the irate customer three packs of another brand. The shopper makes another biting comment, then storms out, looking back at the others, seemingly proud of her rude performance.

Even Hoosiers can, sometimes, be discourteous.

At the west end of the mall is the modernistic Richmond Municipal Building. Tulips are in bloom around much of the building which is across the street from the Wayne County Courthouse. Signs congratulate the Richmond Red Devils state championship teams in basketball (1992), golf (1993) and cross country (1994).

This is a city of sports fans and the home of the Indiana Football Hall of Fame.

A marker south of the mall notes the location of Camp Wayne, a Civil War center where volunteers were organized and trained. It is near an older area of the city with large homes built decades ago.

The tourism bureau calls Richmond "Indiana's great escape" and promotes Wayne as "the world's friendliest county."

Hoosiers take pride in the places they live.

MIDDLEBORO

Status Quo

Ind. 227 turns northeast out of Richmond past a horse farm amid a blend of older and newer homes, then follows the Middle Fork of Whitewater River into the community of Middleboro.

An ancient building, bordered in front with a brick-lined wall, appears to have once been an inn. It is a quiet place, a wide spot in the road, the scenery its most important asset.

Richmond's development to the north has ended and Middle-boro remains much as it has for years.

* * *

Ind. 227 continues due north past scattered suburban homes built on sites sold by farm owners. Only farms and houses are ahead for the next four miles.

WHITEWATER
No Tourist Trap

Whitewater, built around an intersection of Ind. 227 and a Wayne County road, is a town that seems to have kept its residents but not its stores.

A garage is closed, the windows in an old store are boarded and there is no post office. A soft drink machine in front of a private home is the only place to drop money, except for the plates passed around at church.

The school and its athletic teams, the Bears, are gone and students now attend Northeastern High, a consolidation of White-water, Fountain City, Webster and Williamsburg. Despite the union of the four schools at Fountain City, the Northeastern enrollment is only 400, an indication of the rural nature of this part of Wayne County.

* * *

We take a road east of Whitewater a short distance to the Ohio line, then return past a big dairy farm on the banks of the Middle Branch of Whitewater River.

Ind. 227 continues its path north a mile from the Ohio line to the community of Bethel.

BETHEL
An Early Church

In was in Bethel that the first Christian Church north of U.S. 40 was built. A marker notes the lot where the original church was erected in 1821. A new building was completed in 1852 and used as a place of worship until 1894. The building was razed in 1966.

It is not a neat town as most country villages are. The porch of one home is crammed with what appears to be junk. Another house is being razed. A lack of pride of ownership detracts from the homes that are neat and well-maintained.

* * *

Bethel, although it is difficult to imagine because the land is so level, is not far from the highest elevation in Indiana.

The apex of the state is near the Wayne-Randolph County line and the terrain slowly descends from that elevation which is 1,257 above sea level. It is from this area that farms drain in all directions to form the headwaters of eight major rivers, including the White, Wabash, Whitewater and the Big Miami.

We are on top of the state, at least for a short time.

RANDOLPH COUNTY

Established in 1818 and named for Thomas Randolph, a friend and son-in-law of Thomas Jefferson. Population 27,200. Mostly an agricultural county. County seat is at Winchester.

ARBA

A Friendly Place

From Bethel we drive two miles west to Arba Road, a well-paved north-south route past a big dairy farm with Jersey cows. A big home, appearing to be 150 years or so old, has been well maintained.

At the Wayne-Randolph county line the road changes abruptly, the surface no longer smooth. Just to the north is a community marked "Arba — Founded in 1815. Speed limit 30." It is an old neighborhood for this area of the state.

Arba began with the establishment of a Friends Church and soon became the largest settlement in the county. By 1823, the Friends' meeting is reported to have had 276 members.

The church still has a presence in Arba, meeting in a brick and frame church at the south edge of town.

Big homes, one with several acres of neatly-trimmed grass, divided by a gentle creek, show pride of ownership. Some houses have metal roofs from an earlier area.

What once was a store is closed, small retail centers having lost the war of competition with bigger stores in larger towns when the auto came and roads were improved.

As with dozens of other small towns, Arba's past is bigger than its present.

CRETE

Off The Track

Arba Road continues north out of Arba past homes built on a turn in the road. Eight mobile homes are anchored in place.

When the Pennsylvania Railroad sliced through the area, it was Crete's gain and Arba's loss. Crete was a far different place when the train tracks brought passengers into and out of town and picked up and dropped off produce. The rails have been removed, leaving freight to be shipped by truck.

The big grain elevator remains the heart of Crete. A farmer has just pulled onto the scales, his truck loaded with shelled corn.

Nice farm homes surround the area, hinting of the productivity of the farms.

* * *

We are in one of the earliest areas settled in this part of Indiana, a stopping place for families on their way from Pennsylvania and other eastern states.

At the intersection of U.S. 36 and Arba Road, motorists are alerted to "Hidden Drives — Watch for Children."

SPARTANBURG

Home Town Bank

What once was Spartanburg High School, home of the Tomcats, still stands at the south edge of town. The bell tower is in place, but the building appears to be privately owned.

As in most small Indiana towns, students now attend a consolidation, Spartanburg having united with Lynn to form Randolph Southern, a high school with 230 students.

The sign at town limits warns: "Slow — Children at Play." This is obviously a community that cares about its young people. It also is a family town, its Greensfork Township park having assorted playground equipment, a tennis court and shelter house.

Its dead are not forgotten either. At the town cemetery, a 20-foot tall stone monument is dedicated to "the memory of all soldiers and sailors living and dead who served the United States in any of its wars." The monument was erected in 1931, long before the town sent men and women to fight and die in World War II, Korea, Vietnam, Grenada and Desert Storm. An American flag waves on a pole nearby, a silent tribute to those who served.

Most of the houses in town show pride of ownership, but a few do not, but that is the norm in almost any town on "Borderline Indiana." A cream separator in front of one of the homes is a reminder of the day when almost every farm had a few cows and used such a machine to spin the cream from the milk.

Among the few businesses in town is the Greensfork Township State Bank. It is good to see that not all financial institutions are huge multi-state concerns where depositors are known by numbers instead of names.

Spartanburg is a town with a proud history. Just two miles to the northeast is the brick, two-story school that housed the Union Literary Institute. The Friends Meeting, in 1845, established the school which provided grade and high school education for both black and white students.

Indiana: A new Historical Guide reports that 70 percent of the 230 students enrolled in 1849 were black. The students attended class in a log building until the brick school was built in 1860.

The school's enrollment declined after the Civil War and the building was leased as a public school from 1869 until 1908 when pupils were sent to Spartanburg.

Arba Road continues its route to the north through farm land that seems endless in all directions.

BARTONIA
Closed by Progress

Except for a few houses, a church is about all that remains in Bartonia, which is two miles from the state line. A welding shop, where farmers once came to have machinery repaired, is abandoned.

A "Sorry — We Are Closed" sign is posted on a two-story building with a porch across the front. It is a place, no doubt, where farmers swapped stories in the days before cars allowed quick trips to towns and giant superstores made it difficult for neighborhood stores to compete.

The land has turned slightly rolling, the soil less rich, at least for a few miles. An old bridge has a seven-ton load limit, barely strong enough to carry a loaded school bus.

SOUTH SALEM
Four-Way Stop

At first glance, South Salem appears to be a four-way stop at an intersection of Randolph County roads.

It is, however, a busier place on Sunday mornings when residents from miles around attend the Church of Christ, a brick building to which two wings have been added.

Nice houses are near the intersection. A big farm house is on one of the roads. Across from it is a home that looks as if it belongs on a southern plantation, its roof covered with sheets of metal. A third house, a quarter-mile off the road, its lot surrounded by farm land, is well landscaped.

We take Randolph County Road 100 South to Ind. 227, which ends its route to the north at U.S. 32 just south of Union City.

UNION CITY
Two Timing Towns

Union City is a surprise, a bigger, busier town with more stores than we had expected. Few parking spaces remain in the business district on this Friday afternoon.

It is a family community. Old, but well-maintained homes, are on tree-lined, well-paved streets.

Like College Corner, Union City is on the state line, but its business district is in Indiana and 3,625 of its 5,600 residents live on the Indiana side.

But life can be confusing here. Each side of the city has its own municipal government, its own schools, policemen and firemen. And at certain times of the year, clocks on the Ohio side are an hour ahead of those in Indiana. The post office, which serves both sides of Union City, is in Indiana with an Indiana zip code.

Rivalries between the two cities are not always friendly. The joint slogan, "The Hub of Two States," according to the book *Indiana: A New Historical Guide*, is sometimes rephrased to read "the stub of two hates."

Union City kept its high school and its name after school consolidation when students were sent here from Jackson and Wayne Township Schools. The Union City Wildcats, Jackson Bulldogs and Wayne Tigers now are the Union City Indians.

Despite the consolidation, and Union City's population, the total high school enrollment is just over 300, indicating an older population in this area of the state.

Trains no longer stop for passengers in Union City, but what is marked as the "Historic Union City Depot" remains as the home of the Randolph County Art Association. A brick walk at the depot is lighted by street lamps of an earlier time.

Visitors today come not by train but by car. No matter. No one remains a stranger long in Union City. As in other towns, the local Hardee's is a busy restaurant at 7 a.m. on a Saturday morning. It is obviously a place where customers come morning after morning, know each other's names . . . and each other's problems.

Every town needs a community gathering place.

* * *

A blacktop road leads from Ind. 28 north out of Union City toward New Lisbon through farms with rich loam soil. A metal shed stretches beyond the length of a football field, turkeys crowded against its fenced openings, unaware of the destiny that awaits them.

NEW LISBON
Tombstone Territory

Church typical of those on eastern Indiana border

New Lisbon appears to be another tombstone in the cemetery of history. Two graveyards, an older one on the east side of the road, a newer one on the west side, are on the road into the community.

To the north is the New Lisbon Christian Church, built, a marker says, in 1881. The preacher's sermon for Sunday will be "Finding the Courage to Unlock Closed Doors."

This is a peaceful community on the banks of the Little Missississenewa River. There may be few locked doors here in Jackson Township, but chances are the minister will be talking about another kind of lock on a different kind of door.

New Lisbon we soon learn is a half-dozen or so houses surrounded by sizable farms in the distance.

* * *

We make a note that rural southern Indiana towns are more likely to have stores or coffee shops than those in the north where farms are bigger and the distance between homes greater.

* * *

On the road north from New Lisbon, Brahman cattle graze on the lush grass of spring. The land is rich, level, almost unobstructed here on the state line, broken only by drainage ditches needed to remove excess water for streams are few.

Barns are identified with names of the owners, some with the year the family occupied the land. Buildings are in good condition. One farm has all its buildings — the house, two barns, unused chicken house, a shed and some other smaller outbuildings — painted in non-offensive yellow. Up the road is an abandoned farm, its buildings unpainted, their roofs rusted. The house appears to have been damaged by fire; the family gone, leaving another farmer to expand his acreage.

Farms will need to be even bigger to survive as the 21st Century nears.

* * *

Just south of the Jay County line, the terrain begins to turn from flat to slightly rolling. Only the weather changes more often than the landscape in Indiana.

JAY COUNTY

Established in 1835 and named for John Jay, who was a chief justice of the U.S. Supreme Court. Population, 21,500, a third of which is in Portland, the county seat.

SALEM
One of Many

We wonder how many communities in Indiana are named Salem as we enter Jay County and locate another one. There seem to be many. This Salem is rural, built around the intersection of Roads 700 East and 900 South, a ghost of its past.

What was once a garage is closed. A two-story frame building that was a store is now a residence. Another old store is no longer open. Neither is a body shop that is out of business.

"Beware of the dog," a sign says at one of the homes. We do not challenge the warning.

* * *

Farms continue to appear prosperous even though the land is a bit more rolling along the blacktop road north of Salem. Storage bins and silos dot the landscape.

Once again, though, the terrain changes, the land appears more swampy, trees become more numerous. The road changes, too, for the worse. The Jay County Highway Department seems to have forgotten the stretch we are traveling.

Another farm is abandoned, its house without windows, its chicken house and crib collapsing.

SALAMONIA
Lost In Time

It is mid-morning on a spring Saturday and nothing is astir in Salamonia. It is a place that seems lost in time. There is no one on the streets, no place to meet residents, the nearest cup of restaurant coffee is miles away.

Two old-time gas pumps, one a gravity-flow with a 10-gallon glass bulb at the top, remain in front of an abandoned general store. Another building appears to have had three store fronts, but none are open or in business. An "Enjoy Coca Cola" sign hangs out front, but no soft drink is available. It is a sizable residential town with no businesses.

Streets are tree-lined, the houses large. One of the streets appears to have at least 15 homes for sale. A few newer homes are at the north side of town.

The post office is out of business, leaving residents to get their mail from boxes out front. Picking up and posting letters no longer is a social event.

Except for churches, the Jay County VFW Post 2840, one of the nicest buildings in town, appears to be the only other spot for residents to congregate.

The Salamonia Christian Church, which has an open bell tower, and the United Church of Christ are in the residential area. The Lutheran Church is across the road from the town cemetery at the south edge of town. A marker in the graveyard is dedicated to "veterans of all wars" with a reminder, "The memories will never die."

A person sitting in a car in front of one of the churches says he is from Ohio, claims he knows little about the town and declines to reveal what he does know.

We leave him with his thoughts and his privacy. It is one of the few times since our journey began that we have met a cool reception.

We learn later that a proposal to require homes in the area to hook up to a rural sanitary sewer system has divided residents, which may explain the man's reluctance to talk.

* * *

North of Salamonia the road makes a jog around a junk yard, which is a cemetery for rusting trucks, cars, assorted farm machinery and home appliances.

It is in sharp contrast to neat farms, which far outnumber the unsightly ones. Once again giant silos and storage bins dominate the skyline.

We reach Ind. 26 and County Road 700 East, then turn west on Ind. 26 to the Noble Township School, which is now an auto sales lot.

Sonny Sheffer is at work. He's friendly and talkative as he finishes hooking a battery charger on a car and invites us into his garage. He's just back from Florida, catching up on what didn't get done while he was gone. It is obvious he is eager for a conversation.

He talks about health care costs, recalls that five years ago he had a lung that collapsed. "I thought I had gone," he remembers. "It was diagnosed as a heart attack. They gave me aspirin even though I told them I was allergic to it. The aspirin caused internal bleeding, but the tests showed no heart attack.

"Anyhow, the bill eventually came to $76,000 and I had to sell 63 acres to pay for surgery I didn't need. I tell you, I'm not happy with those big hospitals," he says.

He also is unhappy about government restrictions on car sales, dealer plates and other issues. "We need a few more politicians," he says facetiously. "They change things every day," he adds, showing his disgust.

Sonny talks about the Salamonia he once knew. "I used to get my haircuts down there for 20 cents.

"A friend of mine who owns a farm just west of Salamonia spent $8,000 four years ago to put in a new septic tank. Now he has been told he will be required to have it pumped out and filled in, then hook onto a central sewerage system. And he says he'll have to pay $62 a month.

"Government regulations," Sheffer says, his voice trailing off with resignation.

He is not a bitter man, just upset with things that bother him. He is looking forward to another reunion of his Madison Township High School graduating class.

"Last year, I came home from Florida to go to it. It was my 50th (class of 1944). Even though I have gone through some health crises I didn't need, I guess I should count my blessings. I think there were 26 or 28 of us in the class. Of the 10 boys, I'm the only one alive. Only four of the girls have husbands who are still living.

"I guess I should count my blessings," he repeats.

* * *

Sheffer doesn't have a coffee pot on and the closest restaurant is six miles away in Portland. We are greeted there by a "Welcome to Portland — A Place to Grow" sign and more fast food restaurants than we have seen since Richmond.

We return east on Ind. 26, then go north on a paved road, not far from the Ohio border. Except for a house or two and a church, with no denomination indicated, there is little in a place marked on the map as Noble.

The next settlement is five miles to the north. We are in an area of huge farms where only towering silos rise in the distance. Limberlost Creek cuts through the area, indicating we are not far from Gene Stratton Porter country.

TRINITY
Guide For the Lost

The community of Trinity is easy to find. Its church spire shows the way and no one who follows it will be lost.

The steeple, surrounded by scaffolding and under repair, rises more than 100 feet over the flat land that surrounds Trinity Catholic Church, the hub of a farm community on Ind. 67, two miles from the Ohio border.

Built in 1885, the church is on the national register of historic places. A rectory, school, shelter house and playground are on the church grounds.

NEW CORYDON
Jay County's Start

Farms end and a swampy area begins two miles north of Trinity for we are near the headwaters of the Wabash River.

A bridge crosses the river, which is narrow at this point, into a village, identified by a hand-lettered sign: "New Corydon, 1821. Home of the Blue Heron." It was the first settlement in Jay County, we learn.

New Corydon never had a high school, but a small brick school, no longer in use, is marked "1900 — Wabash Township

District No. 2." High school students attend Jay County High School, a consolidation of Bryant, Dunkirk, Madison Township, Gray, Pennville, Poling, Portland and Redkey.

Just north of the school, Little Leaguers are at the baseball diamond with their adult coaches.

It is obvious New Corydon once was a busier place. At Broadway and Main, a garage is abandoned and a store now is closed as are other buildings that appear to have been retail outlets. One building has metal siding, the kind that dates back to the early 1900s.

It is an interesting town. We wish we could rewind the clock and look back on the New Corydon that time has passed, see the blue herons, the buildings when they were newer, the lot at the entrance into town before it was cluttered with junk.

It is from here the Wabash, which has its start in Ohio, runs north to Huntington before beginning its southwesterly course through Indiana.

* * *

To the north is Adams County. We drive to Ind. 116 which makes a 90-degree turn to the north after entering the state from Ohio.

ADAMS COUNTY

Founded in 1836 from a part of Allen County and named for John Quincy Adams, sixth president of the United States. Population 31,100. Mostly agriculture with about 36 percent of its population living on farms.

* * *

North of New Corydon, the land is swampy and surface water covers some areas after a heavy rain. We meet a horse and buggy as we entered the land of Amish and Mennonite.

GENEVA
Limberlost Land

Ind. 116 turns to the west toward Geneva and we take a side trip to Gene Stratton Porter's "Land of the Limberlost." It was at her home here, now a state memorial, that she wrote six novels from 1903 to 1923.

It was a time when Limberlost was an area of forests in a swampy wilderness, which later would be cleared, drained and converted to fertile farm land.

* * *

From Geneva we return east on Ind. 116 and see husbands and wives in horse-towed buggies en route to Geneva. Saturday is still a big shopping day for these folks who make their living from the land.

We pass one harness shop, then another, for horses are both a means of transportation and field work.

Not all residents, however, are Amish. St. Mary's Catholic Church — dedicated October 28, 1883 — is on Adams County Road 700 East.

A PARADOX
Untapped Power

Road signs warn motorists to be alert for horse drawn vehicles. Off the road are Amish houses without wires to power lines. Windmills spin in the spring wind, pumping water from wells, as they have done since before the time of electric power.

The scene is a paradox. Giant electric transmission lines cross the farm country, but the Amish prefer to live life as it was lived in an earlier time when kerosene lighted rural America.

Off the road, a farmer uses a pitchfork to load manure onto a horse-drawn spreader.

On Road 550 east, a mile from the state line, clothes dry in the wind at a plantation-style home. The barn is dated 1894, the name Schwartz painted above it.

At a big dairy farm, cows are hand milked. Mechanical milkers are powered by electricity and the owner will have none of it in his barn.

We have driven five miles without seeing a village, a town, even a cross roads settlement. Jefferson Township in the southeastern section of Adams County has no villages, nor does Blue Creek Township to the north.

It is time for lunch, and we turn east on Ind. 218 toward Berne. A teen-age Amish miss tries to keep away from the bitter wind at a roadside cart from which she is selling bread, apple butter, noodles, cookies, pies, rolls and angel food cakes. The prices are reasonable, $2 for a big loaf of rye bread, $2.50 for pint of apple butter. Both turn out to be worth the cost.

She is pleasant, polite, but answers questions briefly, volunteers no information.

Three buggies are in line as they head toward Berne. Rather than slow traffic, the drivers pull to the side of the roads to let cars pass. Amish coming from Berne return our waves if they haven't greeted us first.

BERNE

A Touch of Europe

"Berne — A Swiss Community" signs greet visitors. The shopping district is a glance back in time to Saturday mornings when all county seat towns were crowded with shoppers.

The first Swiss immigrants settled in Adams County in the late 1830s, but it was not until 1852 that 70 devout Mennonite immigrants came to the area directly from Switzerland. The area where they settled became the town of Berne when the Grand Rapids and Indiana Railroad opened in 1871.

The First Mennonite Church remains a tourist attraction, but most denominations have congregations here, too, which participate in religious activities coordinated by the Berne Ministerial Association.

A number of industries have plants in Berne, but the town is best known for the fine furniture made at two factories.

Despite an increase in tourism business, Berne has somehow escaped the over-commercialization of some other Indiana towns. Restaurants, however, are numerous. We choose the Vinson's Corner Meet'n Haus where the food is good, the atmosphere pleasant and the antiques, collectibles and gifts worth viewing.

* * *

Back near the Indiana-Ohio border Little Blue Creek meanders along the eastern side of Adams County north of Ind. 218. The land remains rich for six miles are so, then turns swampy near the junction of St. Mary's River and Blue Creek.

A stone quarry, its dirt mound rising on the horizon, is near the state line on Ind. 124. Not far away are two oil wells, the first we have seen since leaving southwestern Indiana.

PLEASANT MILLS
"Hanging In There"

Ind. 101 parallels the state line two miles to the east and leads into Pleasant Mills, a community with two conservation clubs nearby.

It is obvious this area on the banks of the St. Mary's River is a sportsman's paradise. The only retail business in town is the Riverside Sports Shop where guns, archery equipment, bait, fishing gear, hunting clothes and ammunition are for sale.

It's also a convenience store, the only one on the entire eastern border of Adams County.

A dated "stop the landfill" notice is on a wall at the store. Luann Rehm, who owns the store with her husband, Rick, explains that the movement to stop the landfill was successful, thanks to the united opposition of area residents.

"It was planned right along the river (St. Mary's). Supposedly the EPA (Environmental Protection Agency) had checked out the site and said it was suitable for a landfill. I said if that's the case, our EPA obviously is not very good.

"They were going to put it (the landfill) in real low land which always floods really bad. The developers claimed they would build that area up so the run off would not enter the river. We said, 'no way.' You don't have to be a rocket scientist to figure out there would be leakage through the sand and gravel."

The defeat of the landfill was a victory for the people of Pleasant Mills and for the sportsmen who visit the town.

The Rehms, who live in Bluffton, have owned the store for 13 years. "I didn't know much about Pleasant Mills until we bought this place, but I learned there once was a blacksmith shop, a number of stores and a grist mill on the river," Mrs. Rehm says.

The town still has its post office, but Eldana Edgell wonders how long it can keep it. She is what is called a postmaster relief, a temporary title she has had since the former postmaster retired three years earlier.

There is concern the U.S. Postal Service might eventually phase out the post office here. "We are sure trying are best to keep it. They haven't closed us yet and we're still hanging on."

The post office, which has 32 boxes but no rural route, is in a 10-by-10 feet addition to the house where the retired postmaster lives. Like other towns, it is a community center of sorts, a place for residents to meet, trade news and retain pride in the place they live.

If the post office closes, Pleasant Mills will lose another bit of its identification. Its high school, whose Spartans generated community spirit during basketball seasons four decades ago, is closed. Students from town now attend Adams Central High School, a consolidation with Kirkland and Monroe near Monroe.

Chances are if the high school remained, a Spartans logo would replace the Chicago Cubs emblem painted on a satellite dish on one lawn in town.

* * *

U.S. 33 which cuts through Pleasant Mills is more heavily traveled now that truckers have found it is a short cut to I-75 in Ohio. But to them Pleasant Mills is just a place to drive through, not a town where people make their homes and work together to make it a better place.

BOBO

Don't Call It Rivare

A dot on an old Adams County map shows Rivare is just north of Pleasant Mills on Ind. 101. The official Indiana highway map says it is Bobo.

No matter. Bobo is a town with marked streets and a number of modest homes. What once was a two-story brick school dating back to 1913 is now privately owned.

Two grizzled-faced men in a car with no muffler, stop at our request. They concede the town may have been known once as Rivare but it has been known as Bobo for years.

"I'm 63 — lived here all my life — and it has always been called Bobo," one of them says as he drives away, the roar of his unmuffled car caught in our tape recorder.

* * *

North of Bobo, a sign reads "Keep and Bear Arms." It is obvious Hoosiers like their guns.

Near the junction of Ind. 224, a business offers "trenching service and laser accurate top soil." We wonder what laser accurate soil is, but there is no one to ask.

We leave Ind. 101 and go north on Adams County Road 500 East. Farms grow larger and once again the land seems boundless.

An Adams County highway worker repairs chuckholes, alone, unlike crews where two or three partners sometimes watch while one works.

The state line is at Road 700 East, but no signs say Indiana or Ohio. That is of no concern. These are the United States of America and border lines primarily are for political and governmental purposes, not to separate residents of one state form another.

Up ahead on the Ohio side, however, is a road marker that does say Ohio-Indiana state line. The view remains almost unrestricted. The paved road continues for several miles between the two states.

ALLEN COUNTY

One of Indiana's most populated counties (300,100 residents, 173,100 of whom live in Fort Wayne, the state's second largest city). Established in 1823. Named for Col. John Allen, an Indian fighter. An industrial, commercial county where agriculture is still important.

DIXON

That's It

Unlike most borders separating counties, the division line between Adams and Allen counties is marked.

Two miles to the north is Dixon, another community which straddles the Indiana-Ohio line. Not much remains in Dixon except for a few houses, most of which are in Ohio. The town will, however, soon have one additional house. A firm identified by a sign out front as "That Construction Company" is erecting the home.

A grain elevator is still in business, but a second one near the railroad is not.

MONROEVILLE

Self Sufficient

We leave the state line and return to Ind. 101 to visit Monroeville, a busy town that seems larger than its 1,250 population.

It is the center of a fertile farm area as evidenced by eight giant silos that tower over the town from its grain elevator.

It is not necessary to wonder about Monroeville's history. It is revealed on a plaque: "Founded 1851 in vast wooded area with many lumber mills and stave and barrel factories. At one time it was the home of author Lloyd C. Douglas. It was here he obtained the incentive to write some of his books, including *Time to Remember, The Big Fisherman* and others."

Monroeville, unlike many smaller towns, has retained its business core. It has a lumber company, auto dealership, restaurants, public library, post office and a barber shop with a genuine barber pole. Large, old homes from an earlier time are numerous.

Monroeville High School no longer exists, but Heritage High School, a consolidation of Hoagland and Monroeville, is near town.

It is good to see that a small town has retained its character in an era of constant change.

* * *

North of Monroeville on Ind. 101 is the hamlet of Townley, a wide spot in the road with an auto shop and bar. The Road House Tavern appears to be busy at mid-morning, having more cars parked out front than the auto shop.

North of Townley the soil remains fertile, the farms large. At one farm a black swan swims on a small pond lined with riprap stone.

Back on State Line Road, an old sycamore stands forlorn, the only tree on a stretch of road lined with productive farms. It is a solitary reminder of a time when the area was a dense forest where open spaces were rare.

The two states appear to have worked in harmony here on the border. Deep drainage ditches run for a time along the Ohio side of the road, at other times on the Indiana side.

* * *

A basketball bounce from the edge of the state, Edgerton is appropriately named.

Chances are it grew up with the railroad that runs west into Fort Wayne and east into Ohio. It is another agricultural community, its major businesses the grain elevator and farm center.

Homes are a mixture of the old and the new in the community on Ind. 14, which goes east to New Haven and Fort Wayne.

WOODBURN

Mayor Herb

The mayor of Woodburn is almost as well known as the city he runs. He is Herb Roemer, who was elected mayor in 1963 and re-elected every four years since.

He is in his mid-70s, arrives at his office each day by 7 a.m., handles what needs his attention, then leaves for his regular job as a salesman in Fort Wayne. He returns to his Woodburn office at night. Meantime, if the need arises, he can be reached via the beeper he wears.

Roemer is from an era when folks stayed close to the place where they were born, did what they could to make it better and saw no need to move elsewhere.

He grew up on a farm a mile from Woodburn, then moved to town. "That's as far as I've gone. I've never lived any place else," he has told others in interviews.

On this day he is at work in Fort Wayne. We have missed him and that is our loss.

This is Indiana's smallest city, the 1990 census setting the population at 1,321. It may not remain small long, however, because new homes are being built around town. Its nearness to Fort Wayne, makes it a prime area for development.

Two miles from the state line, Woodburn is surrounded by flat, fertile farm land, but it no longer is a farm town. It is home of a giant Uniroyal Goodrich factory now owned by the Michelin Tire Company, one of the biggest employers in Allen County.

The old Woodburn High School consolidated with part of Harlan to form Woodlan which is northwest of town.

We leave Woodburn in good hands, the hands of Herb Roemer who has guided the city well.

* * *

There are no more towns near the border in Allen County as we follow county roads to the north, crossing the Maumee River which twists and turns endlessly. The terrain varies, so does the soil, fertile in places, not so rich in others. An airplane is parked near a farm home, its private landing strip in the background.

There are no communities in Scipio Township at the northeast corner of Allen County, only a place on an old map identified as Halls Corner at an Ind. 37 crossing. If it was ever a town, it no longer is. The land has turned rolling, more wooded. We have left an area of huge farms, at least for a time.

An east-west road leads back to Ind. 101 which passes the Deer Run wilderness area. "No fishing allowed," a sign warns.

The Northeast

DEKALB COUNTY

Formed in 1835 and named for Bavarian baron Johann DeKalb, a Revolutionary War general. Population 35,400. Mostly agriculture, although many of the towns have attracted new industry

———

Indiana counties, we have found, have no uniform road marking systems. Many use directions, north, south, east and west, some use numbers, others use names. DeKalb uses two digit numbers, such as Road 56.

As we enter DeKalb, the land does not appear as rich as it did along the state line to the south. Trees and woodlands are more common.

NEWVILLE

On Banks of St. Joseph

Newville, the town, is the only settlement of any size in Newville, the township, in the southeastern corner of the county.

The St. Joseph River runs through the community of 50 or so homes, one of which flies both the American and Confederate flags. Another home has posted double warnings — "No Trespassing" and "Beware of Dog" — for uninvited guests.

There is no post office, no stores. The only competition appears to be between the Methodist Church and the Church of Christ, which is in a grove not far from the river.

* * *

We continue north on Ind. 1, which joins Ind. 101 at Ind. 8. The terrain remains rolling, the farms smaller.

BUTLER

An "Eaten" Place

A French fryer is working overtime at Mom's Eaten Haus on the main business block in Butler at noon on a Thursday. The chorus from nearby Eastside High School is having lunch and most of the teens have ordered cheeseburgers and fries.

It is an orderly group, well behaved, polite and courteous to a busy waitress. The girls have assorted hair styles and dress. So do the boys. One sports a Mohawk cut.

(Eastside is a consolidation of Butler and Riverdale, which was an earlier consolidation of Concord Township and Spencerville. Athletes from Butler who once played as Windmills are now the Blazers.)

A server mentions that it is her first day at work, but she knows the menu, as do most of the customers.

Mom has decorated her "Eaten Place" well, the mementos on the walls reminders of the past that make for conversation in the present. Antique medicine boxes, tools, pictures, programs are on the walls. Old tobacco tins — Velvet, Prince Albert, and others — decorate the men's restroom.

The food is good. It is a stop that has renewed our appreciation of "Mom's" cooking as well as a generation of young people on a passage into adulthood.

Outside, two lonely men sit on steps three stores apart, perhaps wishing back to the time they, too, enjoyed the camaraderie of high school friends.

Butler has two railroads, two major highways, Ind. 1 and U.S. 6, a number of small factories and a population of 2,500. And a bright future, it appears.

ARCTIC
However It's Spelled

Once again the character of the land changes along Ind. 1 north of Butler, the farms bigger, the land richer. We drive east toward the state line and cross Fish Creek.

Maps spell the village on County Road 79 A-r-t-i-c. A small sign south of the railroad identifies it as A-r-c-t-i-c.

No matter! This is not an arctic zone. This Arctic has three houses, one frame, one a manufactured home, one a two-story brick that appears to date back to the founding of the town.

Not many motorists visit Arctic, but there are gates at the crossing which trains pass over without slowing down. Another A-r-c-t-i-c sign is north of the railroad.

* * *

North of Arctic, the terrain changes once again, "glacially rolling," it is called. The road passes an old school, its identity — "Troy Township District 1. Built 1916" — engraved on a stone in the brick front. The tower remains, but its bell has been removed. The school has become a private residence.

STEUBEN COUNTY

Forms northeastern corner of Indiana. Established in 1835 and named for Baron Friedrich Von Steuben, a Prussian-born Revolutionary War hero. Population 27,500. County seat is Angola. Called by tourism promoters as "Home of 101 Lakes."

We drive north on a county road into Steuben County past a giant barn, a style from an earlier time, with two concrete silos. "Walhalla Stock Farm - 1904," a sign proclaims.

The old Wabash Railroad slices from southwest to northeast across Richland Township. Fruit trees are in bloom, nature turning part of a farm into a scene for a color postcard.

A sign on the road, unexplained, points east to "Cliff County — 1,346 miles." We search the atlas, find no Cliff County in the United

States. Somewhere, a jester may be laughing at the conversation piece he has erected.

A sawmill, which is rare in northern Indiana where little timber is cut, is near the road.

ALVARADO

Egg Business

The District No. 1 School, built in 1887, still stands in the corner of a pasture at Alvarado's crossroads, outliving most of the students who entered its doors.

Windows in the brick structure are screened, some panes broken.

The United Methodist Church, its playground equipment on well-mowed grass, welcomes visitors. Alvarado has eight houses and there are no clues that it was ever much larger than a four-way stop at Road 800 East and 500 South.

There is one business, of sorts, in Alvarado. A farm at the north edge of the community offers "Eggs for Sale."

Nearby, a sign warns motorists to be aware of horse drawn vehicles.

* * *

To the north a farmer runs toward his house, leaving his four-horse team tied to a fence, but still hitched to an eight-foot wide cultipacker.

There is no sign of an emergency, so we do not interfere. A short distance away, another team is led toward a barn. Neither electric nor telephone lines reach to the house or the barn. We are once again in the land of the Amish.

Again the land is rolling, the road rising and falling, a reminder of some east-west southern Indiana routes we have traveled earlier. Fields are smaller and more land is in grass than in most northern Indiana counties.

METZ

People Not Things

Metz, three miles north of Alvarado on Road 800 East, has no store. The building where one once operated is now the Metz Apartments.

Closed too is the old Metz High School, which also has a new use and a new label. "Gilbert Farms," a sign says at the school which was home to the Metz Mohawks until students were sent to Angola and Hamilton.

The Metz Christian Church remains as it has since the mid-1800s. "Serving our community for 150 years," a sign out front reads, a notation adding that its sesquicentennial was observed in August 1993.

An orchard up the road appears to be the only place around Metz to spend money.

* * *

Old Road 1 passes under the Indiana Toll Road, I-90, into a wooded area of few homes. The farm lands of northern Indiana have disappeared. Instead of grain crops there are Christmas tree farms. Instead of well-drained farm fields there is mostly swamp land.

YORK

On The Corner

A crossroads community on Old Road 1 with three houses and a United Methodist Church is identified as York.

North of York a goat grazes on grass in a barn lot. Up the road a farm is abandoned, the only sign of life a few chickens pecking through grass for bugs.

A half-mile north of York, the Ohio division ends and Michigan forms the last five miles of Indiana's eastern border.

Another school, a one room brick marked District No. 1, is at the junction of Old Road 1 and Ind. 120. A sign points to "Four Corner Market and Snack Bar" near the northeastern corner of the state.

The terrain is rolling, wooded at times, swampy in places. We drive to Long Lake, part of which is in Indiana, part in Michigan, which is to the east at this point. Clear Lake is to the southwest.

We are in the far northeastern corner of Indiana, as far as the roads can take us. Few roads in the area are improved and we return south to Ind. 120.

HAROLD'S HILTON
Buy, Sell or Trade

Hoosiers are an enterprising lot. Take Harold L. Nelson, "Hubcap Harold," as he's known.

"Hubcap Harold's" farm on the south side of Ind. 120 is the home of thousands of hub caps. "Buy, sell or trade," a sign says.

His office in a barn identified as "Harold's Hilton" is open, but Harold is not around. He is elsewhere on the property. "Blow horn," visitors are advised, but we do not bother Harold for we are interested only in conversation, not in buying, selling or trading.

"Hubcap Harold's" is open seven days a week. Being an entrepreneur is a full-time business.

FREMONT
Good Fortune

The town of Fremont, to the west on Ind. 120, is as proud of its heritage as Harold is of his hub caps.

A historical marker in the business area reveals the town was settled in 1834 as Little Prairie, platted as the village of Brockville in 1837, and renamed Fremont for explorer John C. Fremont when the post office opened in 1848.

Fremont is two miles from Michigan at what was once a meeting place for pioneers on their way west. Ind. 120 generally follows the Vistula Trail which originally ran between Fort Dearborn (later renamed Chicago) and Vistula (which is now Toledo).

At one time Fremont had two hotels, its guests arriving daily on the six passenger trains that ran through town.

Unlike some towns its size, Fremont, population 1,400, has kept its high school, many of its businesses and — most importantly — its identity. Enrollment at the high school, where its sports teams are called the Eagles, remains around 350.

It is too bad every town has not been as fortunate as Fremont.

ANGOLA
A Side Trip South

Angola is seven miles from "Borderline Indiana," but it is worth a side trip on this journey around the state. The Steuben County seat, which has 5,500 residents, was settled by families from New England, New York and Pennsylvania. The Fort Wayne-Coldwater (Mich.) Road and the Maumee Trail (from Toledo) crossed in Angola and Indians are said to have once shopped in town.

A Soldiers and Sailors Monument in the circled center of town honors the county's men who served in the Civil War. It is an impressive memorial, topped by a figure of Columbia and surrounded by four bronze statues which represent the infantry, artillery, cavalry and Navy.

The county seat, a New England style courthouse, is to the southeast of the monument.

Angola is near the center of the county close to Pokagon State Park and numerous resort lakes. It is a busy commercial center, especially in summer months.

POKAGON STATE PARK
Snowy Descent

Pokagon is another pearl among the gems that form Indiana's state park system. Off I-69 four miles north of Angola and three miles south of Michigan, it borders on Lake James and Snow Lake.

Visitors can boat, swim and fish. Those who dare may travel at speeds up to 35 to 40 miles per hour down a quarter-mile toboggan track, which is open from Thanksgiving through February.

The park's Potawatomi Inn is open year-round, the indoor pool, sauna, whirlpool and exercise room are available to guests. The dining room on the upper level overlooks scenic Lake James.

* * *

Fireworks outlets are numerous near the Michigan line, opportunists catching motorists from other states at the I-69 and I-90 interchange. Bait shops are common, too, this being the land of lakes.

JAMESTOWN
And Hap's Tap

It is early morning and Hap's Tap, a restaurant and bar on Ind. 120 west of I-69, is serving breakfast. It is a neighborhood gathering spot where most customers know each other, but that doesn't stop them from greeting a stranger.

The food comes with conversation, the topics on this day the weather, home mortgages and fishing. Hap is wearing a T-shirt and overnight growth of whiskers, which will come off once the breakfast crowd has departed.

We ask directions to Jamestown. A waitress says she isn't familiar with the town, then adds, after Hap points the way, "I've been there. But I never knew what it was called." It is that way in rural areas near lakes.

We find Jamestown Road, which is west of Hap's Tap, and drive north, going under I-90. The route leads to Jamestown, a resort community on Lake George, which extends north into Michigan.

Several dozen homes are on the lake, but there are few retail outlets. The meat market is no longer in business. Tom's Donut Shop is open only on Saturdays and Sundays when weekend residents are around. "Milk, bread, T shirts, sweat shirts and bait," a sign reads, with a notation the store may be open daily later in the summer.

We discover we have left our cap at Hap's Tap. We return there, pick it up and are sent away again with "good luck" wishes.

* * *

A few miles west, we see another "Tom's Donut Shop" sign pointing to another lake to the south. Tom knows those who live and fish on the lakes like their doughnuts.

This is one of the state's busiest resort areas. Camping spots are numerous near the Michigan border where the land is more suitable to people than to crops.

Only senior citizens remember one-room schools like the brick one on the south side of Ind. 120. Collins School, serene among oak trees, was used from 1877 to 1943. The brick building was restored in 1967 with 19-century furnishings and remains well maintained.

It is another monument in the graveyard of memories.

NEVADA MILLS

Garage Sale Day

Road 450 West leads south from Ind. 120 to the old town of Nevada (pronounced New-vay-da by some folks) Mills.

It is a busy place this day. Dozens of cars are parked near a church where a community garage sale is under way; garage sales and Fridays being synonymous in Indiana.

Nearby, a brick building identified as "District 4, Jamestown School," is now a private home.

The grist mill on Crooked Creek has long since disappeared, but the dam still controls the levels of Snow Lake, Lake James and Jimerson Lake, which are nearby. To the southeast of town a number of homes are on Clear Creek, above Jimerson.

* * *

The land isn't as good, the fields are smaller, and big farm operations are exceptions in this section of the county where recreation is a bigger industry than agriculture.

We are in an area where visitors can observe nature that remains undisturbed. The Ropchan Memorial Nature Preserve, south of Ind. 120 west of Nevada Mills, is an example. It is a nonprofit 77-acre reserve with woods, swamps, bogs and a small glacial lake.

The preserve is a fast rewind of history, a reminder of what the area once was like. It is in sharp contrast to a junk yard, now known by the politically correct as an auto salvage business, to the west on Ind. 120.

A few Christmas tree farms are off the road on land less suited to grain production.

ORLAND

A Little Vermont

A hint of New England remains in Orland, a town of 415 on Ind. 120 at the west edge of Steuben County on Fawn River. It is believed to be the oldest settlement in the county.

Orland's first settlers in 1834 were from Vermont, church folk who included congregational singing in their worship. It is said residents agreed that Colonel Chapin, the choir leader, would open the hymn book at random and the town would be named after the song on that page. The tune he turned to was "Orland."

The Vermont Settlement Festival is held here each year over the last weekend in July. It is an event that includes buckskinners and their encampments, black powder shoots and outdoor entertainment.

Potawatomi Indians once hunted the lands around Orland, which legend says was a thoroughfare on the underground railroad. Residents helped blacks escape their masters, just three decades after white men drove the Indians from the scene.

Despite its size, Orland is an active place with a grain elevator, a business area, at least two small factories, a post office and Jenkins Junction, a restaurant and bar which is a respite for motorists who pass through town on Ind. 120 and Ind. 327.

Orland High School, whose teams were known at times as the Tigers, on occasions as the Trojans, is now part of Prairie Heights near Lagrange.

Despite the loss of the school, Orland remains a proud community with wide maple-lined streets and well kept homes. It is a model for other towns to follow.

* * *

Lagrange County is a mile to the west. We have traversed the 32-mile border that separates Steuben County from Ohio and Michigan.

LAGRANGE COUNTY

Established in 1832 and named for Marquis de Lafayette's home near Paris. Population 29,500. County seat is at Lagrange. As in Steuben, glacial lakes are numerous. The lakes, farms and forests cover 85 percent of the county, but manufacturing has become more important in recent years.

GREENFIELD MILLS

Down By Mill Stream

It is the surprises that make Indiana a great place to explore. Add Greenfield Mills to that list.

Greenfield Mills is a two-mill operation amid a dozen or so houses around a millpond on Fawn River two miles north of Ind. 120 and a half-mile south of Michigan.

Water first powered a sawmill here in 1834 before the grist mill was added in 1846.

Dan Rinkel, the fourth generation of Rinkels to run the mill, is grinding grain and sacking New Rinkel flour. He's alone and busy but he still greets us warmly, tells us to look around the mill. It's an opportunity too good to pass.

Prices for an assortment of flour, made from various grains for a number of purposes, are written on a blackboard. It is a look back in time, back to the 1940s when almost every farm village had a mill with grain and flour prices scribbled on a slate.

The mill is seeking recipes for which New Rinkel flour can be used. "Please share them with us," a note says.

Stairs lead to the third floor where 50-foot long hand-hewn beams stretch the length of the mill. They are from giant trees that grew in the area when white settlers occupied the land. The trees were God's creation. The mill is a testimony to the work pioneers were able to accomplish with primitive equipment.

Greenfield Mills — A landmark since 1834

The setting is serene, peaceful, much as it likely has been since those early settlers first arrived. Swans can be seen at times on the pond and white sand cranes make their homes nearby.

Dan Rinkel has a chance to talk about the mill, the Rinkel family and about New Rinkel flour:

"Dad (Howard) is president, I'm vice president, Mom (Helen Lee) is secretary-treasurer and the boss." He pauses, then adds, "My sister, Joyce, writes the checks, so maybe she's the boss. We're all family. We (he and his sister) are fourth generation. Our two brothers aren't in the business.

"We have another mill (in the same complex) which grinds flour for organic marketing throughout the country."

Dan's "great gramps," as he calls him, bought the mill in 1904 when the building was billed as "Indiana's greatest dance hall."

"All the milling equipment had to be replaced. My dad and my granddad went around to all the mills that had gone belly up. There were 200 and some here in Indiana at that time. Now only 12 such mills remain in operation in the United States," Dan explains.

Since the 1920s the mill's water power has been supplemented by self-generated hydro-electricity which also is sold to 11 homes in the area, most of which are around the millrace. It is the last of the tiny power companies in the state.

The Rinkels read the meters, mail out the bills and keep the power flowing. They have avoided control by federal and state regulators. "As a privately-owned dam, we don't need a license so we aren't controlled."

The state apparently has no objection. It has helped protect the mill from over-regulation. Even governors of the state have been known to stop to check on the mill when in the area.

Dan fears in this summer of 1995 the future of the millpond. An injunction has blocked lagoons, which would dump into Fawn River, from being built near Orland. An appeal, however, is pending.

"That would turn our millpond into the third lagoon," Dan insists. "We think it should be stopped because there are five endangered species in the river. The only one anyone talks about, though, are some kind of rattlesnakes. The Isaac Walton League has property along the river, a quarter mile from where Orland wants to dump. They have white sand cranes, which are almost extinct. I have a set of swans on my pond which are protected."

Dan Rinkel can look across the millpond to his house where he has added a small mill wheel. "I'm a commercial photographer (as well as a miller) and I needed some sort of logo." The mill wheel is both a conversation piece and a trademark for Dan Rinkel's sideline, "professional photography — commercial, portrait, proms — specializing in weddings."

It has been a pleasant visit.

It is too bad there is no sign out of Ind. 120 to tell motorists about Greenfield Mills. It is a place more people should know about.

* * *

We drive south on County Road 1000 East, cross Ind. 120 and reach the Pigeon River state fish and wildlife area.

It is the state's largest nature preserve, its 11,500 acres stretching 12 miles along the river. It was here that giant Canadian geese were reintroduced to Indiana in 1954.

Quiet, scenic trails lead through an area that has been restored to what nature intended it to be.

Also in the area is the Curtis Creek state trout station, a cold-water hatchery for rainbow and brown trout used to stock lakes and steams.

It was along this area of Pigeon River that hydro-electric dams once operated at Mongo, Nasby and Ontario.

MONGO
Big Squaw Prairie

Add Mongo to the list of unexpected treasures found on this expedition around Indiana. Its place in the state's history is almost as important as that of some Ohio River towns.

It was here French fur traders bartered with the Potawatomi Indians, who called the outpost "Mongoquinong," an Indian term for Big Squaw Prairie or White Squaw.

And it was here on the Pigeon River where settlers built a dam which formed a millrace where a grist mill and distillery once operated. The dam and millpond remain, a tranquil setting for a fisherman who lets his mind roam wherever it will as he waits for a bite.

Closed, however, is the old Mongo Hotel, a two-story frame building on County Road 300 North. "No Trespassing," the signs out front warn.

What may be Mongo's oldest building stands, as it has since 1832, at the northeast corner of the main intersection. The two-story frame was the settlement's first general store and post office.

Across the street is Sarge's, a tavern in a brick building that once was the Mongo State Bank. Sarge's once was a popular spot, but a resident now laments, trying to hide any prejudice: "It is mostly frequented by Mexican-Americans now. A lot of them live near here, some up on Michigan border, some down at Ligonier."

An inn has opened in another old frame building at the southwest corner. "Stage Coach Stop — Bed and Breakfast," a new sign reads. It is too early to determine if it will succeed.

A busy convenience store, cars at its gas pumps, is on the northwest corner.

Berne Garlets is across the way with his dog. "You walking the dog or is he walking you?" we ask.

He looks at the dog. "I'm trying to get him to take me home, but he's in no hurry."

Garlets has other plans than walking the dog. He looks across the way at the town cafe. "Restaurant," a sign says, no name posted. It in a two-story, 100-feet-long building that once was a hardware store, the kind where the owner lived on the second floor.

But back to Garlets. "They are having spaghetti for lunch and I'm going to make it a point to be there. They have a good spaghetti cook," he says, almost convincingly enough to cause a tourist to stay in town longer.

Garlets notes the changes around him. "When I was a kid there were three stores in town and all three did well. Back then there were four farms in the area where one is now. Farmers have to have four times as much ground today to make ends meet," he says.

His observation is correct, a trend to bigness that has reshaped Indiana agriculture, not only along its border but throughout its interior as well.

Small farms will not return. Nor likely will the grist mill, the barber shop, the pool parlor or the meat market Garlets remembers from his youth.

At the Mongo post office, Postmaster Lily Jagoda cares for potted plants when not busy sorting mail or serving customers. She also hands out candy to children who accompany their parents on their daily stops.

She also listens to the woes of residents who do not hesitate to share their problems. A small town is family; one person's misfortune is every one's tribulation. And one's happiness is a joy to all.

We stop at the Mongo Church to add another line to our collection of ministerial comments: "If you are out of harmony with God, guess who changed his tune."

BRIGHTON
Saints Marched Out

A road leads northwest from Mongo to Brighton, where the terrain levels and large farms surround the town at Ind. 3 and Ind. 120.

Little remains in Brighton except its past. A service station is out of business, so is a garage. There is no post office.

The old Brighton High School, once the home of the "Wildcats," is now the Maranatha Christian Fellowship building. Brighton teens have attended consolidated Lakeland High with students from Lagrange, Lima and Wolcottville since the mid-1960s.

It was at Brighton that a commune called the Congregation of Saints was formed in 1843. It considered social and political systems to be in conflict with the principles of Christianity and called contemporary society "little more than pandemonium." It called for the Golden Rule to be fulfilled and agreed to secure the rights and extend the privileges to women.

Like other communes, the experiment at Brighton, soon failed.

Northeast of Brighton is the Camsco Products Plant where mushrooms and other ingredients are processed for Campbell soups.

ONTARIO
Don't Be Sarcastic

Ontario, two miles south of Ind. 120 on Road 225 East, is another Pigeon River town with a dam and history of its own.

Ontario once had flour mills and factories which made wool and other items and tanned leather. It was the home of the Lagrange Collegiate Institute which closed about 1880.

The Ontario of the 1990s has an open square, which is now a park owned by the Ontario Park Association. It is a quiet residential community with no businesses, no post office.

A school built in 1885 (now privately owned) remains as does a New England style church, with no indication of its denomination. Its bulletin board advises those who read it: "The sarcastic thing you leave unsaid will not come back to haunt you."

* * *

We return to Ind. 120 and drive west. The land flattens, the soil turns darker, richer in color. The farms grow larger.

HOWE

Neat And Orderly

It is obvious the people of Howe take pride in their homes. The drive into town from the east is one of the neatest, most graceful we have seen on this odyssey.

It also has more businesses than most towns its size, its population listed as 600. A supermarket, bank and ice cream store are among businesses that line the town square, which has a shelter house, playground equipment and basketball court.

The Town Square Restaurant is busy at noon on this Thursday. It is obvious many of the diners are from out of town, the food and pastries — especially its cinnamon rolls — being known across much of northern Indiana. The restaurant is clean, its decor pleasing, the service good, the food worth a stop even though the tables are a bit cramped.

On the east side of the square near the restaurant is the two-story Kingsbury House which once was a hotel. It now is occupied by business offices.

The Howe Military School, an institution here since 1884, is at the north edge of town. Now open to both male and female cadets, the campus is manicured, the buildings well-maintained. The 190-student high school is a member of the Indiana High School Athletic Association and its teams compete as the Cadets.

Lima-Brighton elementary school is in town, Lima being the name of the community before it became Howe in 1909.

SEYBERTS

A Name But No Town

Maps show "Seyberts" to be south of Ind. 120, a few miles west of Howe and south on Road 450 West from the Marion Mennonite Church. "Visitors Expected," the sign says, indicating the Mennonites are not a closed society.

The road leads to a "T" intersection, but no town. A black-clad Mennonite woman who appears to be in her early 30s stops the bicycle she is riding in the light rain.

She explains we are in what is Seyberts, although there is no town, just scattered farm houses. The house where she now lives was a store, "but that was at least 15 years ago," she explains.

As she talks another woman rides by on a bike. The women are not leery of outsiders in this area where strangers are considered neighbors.

It is an area of good farm land. Huge draft horses, still a source of farm power, are enjoying a day off because of the rain.

The houses have no garages, but residents have no cars, no need for places to park them. Once again we see warnings for motorists to watch for horses and buggies.

SCOTT

By The Mill Stream

Scott is easier to locate than Seyberts. It's two miles to the east, a mile north of Ind. 120 on Road 675 West. Michigan is a mile to the north.

Scott, too, is on Pigeon River and the site of Scott Mill Park, operated by the Lagrange County Park Department in cooperation with the Indiana Department of Natural Resources. It is a public fishing area with a wooden covered bridge for pedestrians.

No town limit signs are posted, but the Scott Methodist Church and the Scott Cemetery indicate we are indeed in Scott.

An old store is closed. The Van Buren Township community building, which appears to also have been a store, is now a scavenger service center.

No school remains. Scott High School, once the home of the Bulldogs, merged with Shipshewana and Topeka to form Westview High.

* * *

Back on Ind. 120 the farms grow bigger, the fields more expansive in this northwest corner of Lagrange County. Three silos tower over a Holstein dairy farm.

SHIPSHEWANA

In Search of the Dollar

From Ind. 120, Ind. 5 leads two miles south to Shipshewana. It is soon obvious we are headed to a small town that has been overtaken by commercialization.

Roadside signs lure tourists to gift shop, antique shops, bed and breakfast homes, country store and restaurants. In town, buildings without character overshadow places like the Davis Hotel where specialty shops are now located.

Shipshewana, once a quiet town of 500, has become a lure for tourists. Antique buyers arrive each Tuesday and Wednesday during warm months to attend flea markets and auctions.

Amish farmers share the streets and parking lot with visitors. But the drive for the dollar has changed the character of the town, robbed it of its genuineness, quaintness and serenity. The people who call Shipshewana home are the losers, or so it seems to an outsider.

The town of today is far different than the one Chief Shipshewana, the Potawatomi chief, knew. The chief was removed from the area in 1838 by federal officials, but allowed to return before he died in 1841.

Away from the tourist attractions, a horse is tethered to a hitching rack. A buggy slows traffic. The grain elevator is in operation. It is good to see some reminders of rural authenticity remain among the commercialization.

* * *

Back on Ind. 120 windmills spin in the wind at houses without electricity, a different world than the pursuit of pleasure back in Shipshewana.

* * *

Two men are fishing in the rain at Stone Lake, a year-around home for a few residents, a weekend retreat for dozens of other families.

The men disagree on the fishing. "Never catch anything here," one says. The other disagrees, "This is usually a good spot," says the other. They are neighbors, full-time residents, two men who likely would rather argue than fish, anyhow.

Stone Lake is at the Lagrange-Elkhart County border, north of Ind. 120 on a paved road. Michigan is a half-mile to the north.

To The North

ELKHART COUNTY

Established in 1830s. Named for the Elkhart Indians who once occupied the area. One of state's most populated counties with a population of 156,200. Largest cities are Elkhart (43,700) and Goshen (23.800), the county seat. Second largest county in size with considerable farm land remaining despite heavy industrialization.

MIDDLEBURY

Beating the Chains

Ind. 13, which crosses Ind. 120 on its way to the state line, leads south five miles to Middlebury, a town of 2,000 residents.

Downtown, Varns and Hoover is a reminder of hardware stores of the past, having escaped the trend that has caused neighborhood businesses to lose out to giant chains. An Amish woman looks through the rows of plants, searching for flowers to set, this being spring and a time of rebirth.

Across the street is the Cinnamon Stick, a Victorian type store. Antique shops are numerous in Middlebury.

It is a neat, orderly town, a business center for eastern Elkhart County. Both businesses and homes show pride of ownership.

This is one of the county's main centers for the manufacture of recreational vehicles.

* * *

We return to Ind. 120 and proceed north past the Indiana Toll Road (I-90) to Elkhart County Road 2, which parallels the state line, a half-mile south of the border. Irrigation equipment is in fields, the soil now muck instead of loam.

The Patchwork Quilt Country Inn is on Road 2 near Vistula, "fine country dining, bed and breakfast," a tourist magazine says. It would be difficult to argue the claim for a number of cars are still out front at mid-afternoon. Lunch is served from 11 a.m. to 2 p.m., dinner from 4:30 to 8 p.m. The restaurant is closed on Sundays and holidays.

Ind. 2 follows the interstate as it dips south. Fields are small, the land swampy among woodlands, Christmas trees being a major crop.

Vistula is a residential area centered around the Vistula Christian Church and an apartment building.

BONNEYVILLE MILL

By the Mill Stream

Down on Little Elkhart River, a half-mile south of Ind. 120 on County Road 131, Bonneyville Mill remains as it has since it was built in 1832.

The mill is a centerpiece in Bonneyville Mill County Park which is a peaceful place to picnic, hike, sled or ski cross country. Or to relax, enjoy the perennial gardens and listen to song birds or the creaks of an old-fashioned wooden windmill break the silence.

Every county should have a county park this impressive.

BRISTOL

No More Vaudeville

Bristol, population 1,250, appears to have more jobs than people to fill them. Factories as well as restaurants have "help wanted" signs.

Bristol is known for its Opera House, a frame building erected in 1892, as a vaudeville theater. It now is used by an Elkhart civic theater group for weekend productions.

Worth noting, too, is St. John of the Cross Episcopal Church (circa 1850s), its ash lumber secured with pegs. A number of other buildings also date back to the town's early years.

Little Elkhart River flows into the St. Joseph River here, three miles from the Indiana-Michigan line. Congdon Park, on the St. Joseph, is well-manicured, large for a town this size.

Bristol remains a thriving community despite the loss of its high school. Students now attend Elkhart Central High.

* * *

The Indiana Toll Road has cut off access to Indiana's northern border. We take the toll road for the first time at the Bristol exchange on Ind. 15.

An interstate is not a good place to see the real Indiana, but few east-west roads are open along the border two miles to the north.

The land is flat across northern Elkhart County. Housing developments are under construction off Ind. 19 north of the city Elkhart. So are new factories. A big dairy farm is off the road but much of the terrain is wasteland.

* * *

Elkhart and Goshen have their own attractions, but this is a look at Indiana's border so we continue west.

ST. JOSEPH COUNTY

Established in 1830. Named for the St. Joseph River. Population 247,200, fourth largest in state, with heaviest concentration in the South Bend-Mishawaka area. County seat is at South Bend, home of Notre Dame University, Studebaker Museum and the new College Football Hall of Fame. The South Bend/Mishawaka Convention & Visitors Bureau aggressively promotes the area.

HARRIS TOWNSHIP
And Growing Granger

It is obvious, even from the Indiana Toll Road, that the area is growing. Hundreds of new homes have been built and are being built in Harris Township which forms the northeast corner of the county.

Ind. 23 exits the toll road and turns northeast toward Granger, a half-mile from Michigan. Granger is no longer the sleepy spot it once was. It is, instead, Boom Town 1990s.

New housing surrounds the town, its core now filled with commercial enterprises, a strip mall, supermarket and new stores under construction.

We no longer have the luxury, as we have had in most border towns, to relax and observe the roadside. We have reached an area of the state where residents are on the move and in a rush to get there. Roads are more crowded, the population more dense.

* * *

The northern boundaries of South Bend are less than three miles from the Michigan border in Clay and German Township, separated by the St. Joseph River. Both townships also are growing rapidly.

To the west is Warren Township, a land of lakes which have names like Mud, Deer and Clear.

* * *

The U.S. 31 bypass skirts South Bend to the west and leads to U.S. 20. The pace of development is slower although a few industrial plants are along the route. Big farms with muck soil are sharp contrast to the urban sprawl back to the east.

HAMILTON
Retirement Living

A county road leads north from the crossroads of Plainfield to Hamilton, a small town, two miles south of the state line.

Hamilton is a small community dominated by Hamilton Grove, a large senior citizen's center with areas for independent living and assisted care. It is a quiet setting in a remote, wooded area far from pollution, traffic congestion and urban noise.

The complex has been affiliated with the Methodist and United Methodist churches since its first building opened in 1922 as the Haven Hubbard Memorial Home. Visitors are invited to the annual ox roast the fourth Saturday of each August.

There is no store, no post office, little other activity in Hamilton. A farm at the edge is for sale, so are burial plots in the cemetery behind the New Prairie Christian Fellowship Church.

NEW CARLISLE
Staying On Track

New Carlisle could be in any county in Indiana for it is more rural than urban, a sharp contrast to bigger, busier South Bend to the east.

Its business district appears unchanged from decades earlier.

U.S. 20 turns through a graffiti-marred viaduct and enters the town from the east. A sign greets visitors: "Welcome to New Carlisle. National Register of Historic Places."

A grain elevator rises along the railroad, this being a farming community that prospered when the South Shore Railroad was routed through town, bringing Chicago area residents to hotels on nearby Hudson Lake.

The Methodist Collegiate Institute, built in 1861, was transferred to the town and now is the site of a park.

New Carlisle joined Rolling Prairie during school consolidation to form New Prairie High School, a system that includes parts of both St. Joseph and LaPorte counties.

LAPORTE COUNTY

Established in 1832. Its name LaPorte is French for "the door" and is believed to reflect the county's access to Lake Michigan. Population 107,000. County seat is LaPorte, its largest city Michigan City.

HUDSON LAKE
Stage Coach Stop

Once called Lac du Chemin, Hudson Lake was home to a number of Mormon families before their moves to Illinois and later Utah.

The lake, just west of the LaPorte-St. Joseph County line two miles south of Michigan, was on the route between Detroit and Chicago in the early 1800. Stage coaches passed through the area on regular runs. Some travelers stayed, built homes and made their livelihood from the rich soil and dense woodlands.

Hudson Lake once was a summer resort for vacationers who traveled from Chicago on the South Shore.

* * *

We drive north of Hudson Lake to LaPorte County Road 1000 which crosses the county a half mile south of the Michigan border. Our destination is the community of Hesston, but we find the 14-mile stretch holds its own secrets, its own history, its own attractions.

A one-room school (1890) now used as a parsonage for the Maple Grove United Methodist Church is at County Road 650 east. The church, one of the oldest in the county, is said to be furnished with the same pews, chairs and lectern used when it opened in 1867.

Further to the west is Posey Chapel Hill, a cemetery whose elevation provides a panoramic view of the countryside.

HESSTON

A Dining Place

The Hesston Bar may be a secret to folks outside the area, but not to LaPorte County residents. It is known for its prime rib and steaks and is open seven nights a week.

It is at the main intersection in Hesston, a small community on County Road 1000, a place diners can come to escape the cities to the west.

Chances are visitors to the bar will find humor in two nearby frame buildings. Made to appear like frontier structure, one is marked "The Livery — 1991" and the other "Hesston Carriage Company — 1987." They were built to be part of the Hesston Carriage Company's country gift shop which does not now appear to be open.

The Hesston Gardens and St. Paul's Monastery are at the north edge of Hesston.

* * *

West of Hesston on Road 1000 is the Galena District No. 2 School, a brick building erected in 1892. The school is now owned by the Steam Society which operates the museum across the road.

The Hesston Steam Museum's collection of steam engines rivals any of its kind. Authentic steam machines, from the thresher and sawmill to the cider press, are in working order.

It is at the museum where Whistle Stop Days are observed over Memorial Day weekends. A North-South Civil War musket and cannon skirmish is fought the second weekend in August. The Hesston Steam and Power show is held on Labor Day weekends. All are annual events.

After Labor Day, visitors can view the fall foliage from aboard one of the antique locomotives that chug through 155 acres of meadows and woods.

Road 1000 North is an area of varied land uses, Christmas trees, horse stables and beef cattle. Blueberries, raspberries, cherries, apples, peaches, apricots and grapes are among the crops raised.

As the route nears U.S. 12 the roadside becomes more wooded, swampy, the land more marginal. Lake Michigan is just ahead.

LONG BEACH

Stylish Comfort

This is not the usual lake side resort. This is luxury — big bucks style — here in Long Beach on Lake Michigan. Many of the homes in the town of 2,300 were designed by John Lloyd Wright, a son of Frank Lloyd Wright, and accent the sand dunes with natural-colored stucco and wood shingles. Multi-level homes blend into the hilly terrain that rises above the lake.

Long Beach was developed as a weekend retreat for Chicago's elite who came to escape the city's heat and legend claims the town was used as a hide-out for 1920-era Chicago gangsters like Al Capone and Bugsy Malone. The "summer cottages," if these expensive homes can be called cottages, remain as examples of architectural splendor.

Long Beach still appears to be summer home to many Chicago residents. Cars parked at homes with private beaches have more Illinois than Indiana license tags.

Huge homes away from the lake front are on wide streets that wind over rolling terrain. The town has its own government, its town hall blending into the architecture of the area.

MICHIGAN CITY

"A Great Hometown"

Lake side homes are less expensive along Lake Shore Drive as it enters Michigan City. What appear to be expensive condominiums — "villas" a sales sign calls them — are being built on the water.

Michigan City's Washington Park, which first opened in 1892, is on the lake front, a place for relaxation, picnicking and a swim from the sandy lake side beach.

It also is the location of the city's zoo, where mammals, birds and reptiles may be seen. The promoters boast: "Wooded grounds and winding trails set against the sand dunes can turn a trip to the zoo into an adventure safari."

A tower built in 1933 by employees of the Works Progress Administration remains open and is a good vantage point to view the southern tip of Lake Michigan from the Michigan shoreline to the Chicago skyline.

Nearby, a short hike from the parking area, is the Old Lighthouse, still used as a sentinel by the U.S. Coast Guard, its lantern seen by captains up to 15 miles away. The restored lighthouse is used by the Michigan City Historical Society as a museum, which preserves the legends and lore of the lake.

Adjoining the park is the Michigan City Marina, where hundreds of pleasure craft are moored. At the pier, two teen-agers cast for fish a few feet away from two senior citizens, the past and the present united in a sport as old as man.

At the main entrance to the park and marina is the Civil War Memorial, a stone shaft, perhaps 30 feet high, erected "in memory of the soldiers who gave their services to perpetuate the union of the states."

To the south along Trail Creek, which empties into the lake, are luxury apartments and condominiums, which form a good first impression for visitors entering the city from the northeast. Not far away is the well-designed government center, neat, attractive, accentuating the "Welcome to Michigan City — What A Great Hometown" banners along the streets.

Not far away is a NIPSCO generating plant. This is industrial northeastern Indiana and industry and recreation have learned to co-exist out of necessity.

MT. BALDY

Shifting Sands

Mt. Baldy rises 123 feet above Lake Michigan

We leave Michigan City on U.S. 12, which changes from a nice highway to a narrow two-lane road in need of repaving.

The beachfront changes quickly from recreation to industry.

Not far from Michigan City is the first section of the Indiana Dunes National Lakeshore. It is here visitors can see Mt. Baldy, the tallest living sand dune on the southern shore of Lake Michigan.

It is a popular attraction and, at times, the parking areas are filled. Mt. Baldy is evidence that Hoosiers sometimes do not appreciate the treasures around them. On this Monday there are more out-of-state cars — Ontario, Missouri, Ohio, New Jersey, Illinois — than Indiana vehicles.

A giant mound of sand rises 123 feet to form Mt. Baldy, northwest winds shifting it inland 45 feet a year, slowly burying the forest in its path.

A short walk through fine, silty, golden-colored sand leads to Mt. Baldy which can be scaled on foot or ascended through steps to the north. The trails near the mound are lined with ferns, poison ivy and Merram Grass, which thrives despite the arid sandy soil.

Lake Michigan now dips into Indiana. Porter County is ahead.

The Northwest

PORTER COUNTY

Established in 1935 and named for Commander David Porter, a naval officer who participated in key battles in the war of 1812. Northern tip of county on Lake Michigan. Population 130,000. County seat is Valparaiso.

SAND DUNES
And Lakefront Towns

U.S. 12, called "the Lake Michigan Circle Tour," follows the edge of Lake Michigan through wasteland as it enters Porter County.

TOWN OF PINES: Not far from the county line is the Town of Pines, one of a number of communities that are on the lake between Michigan City and Gary.

The Town of Pines warns would-be trouble makers that they are being observed by "Community Watch Citizens."

BEVERLY SHORES: A community of 900 residents, some of whom have a Lithuanian heritage from earlier generations. Residents boast that Lakeview Park in Beverly Shores is an ideal spot to watch a stunning sunset on the lake.

Five elegant residences that were moved by barges to Lake Front Drive in Beverly Shores after the 1933-34 Chicago World's Fair remain.

Except for the lake, Beverly Shores is surrounded by park land, leaving the town no room for growth. Lake Front drive follows the beach to State Park Road which is the east border of Indiana Dunes State Park.

TREMONT: A resort community on U.S. 12 that from all appearances is now a part of history.

DUNES STATE PARK: Ind. 49 leads off U.S. to the state park past a historical marker near the site of Le Petit Fort. It was there on December 5, 1780, that American troops engaged in battle with British forces. It was not a major battle, but like hundreds of others it did play a role in America's fight for independence.

The park's beach and its proximity to heavily populated cities make the Dunes one of the state's busiest parks. At least 10 cars are waiting in line to pay entry fees on a Monday morning in early summer. The visitors are here to use the golden-colored beach that stretches out for three miles along the Lake Michigan shore.

There is more, however, than swimming at the park. Nature trails explain the history of the dunes and reveal a variety of desert plants, giant wood ferns and white pines. The park's entire 1,800 wooded acres south of the beach are open for exploration and enjoyment.

INDIANA DUNES NATIONAL LAKESHORE: The federal lands cover 14,000 acres in locations across 18 miles of the Lake Michigan shoreline. An estimated 1,500 species of plants, from arctic barberry to cactus, may be found on park land.

A move to protect a total of 45 miles of shoreline on the Lake in LaPorte, Porter and Lake Counties is the center of debate about government control over private property.

Opponents call the plan intrusive, costly and a threat to their right to use property as they see fit. Others note that the plan isn't complete, and that public input is still being sought. The disagreement centers over whether Indiana should apply for a voluntary federal program that provides funding for coastal improvement.

Porter County commissioners opposed the plan, saying it would increase deficit spending and government bureaucracy.

PORTER BEACH: One of a number of beaches on land that is a part of the Indiana Dunes National Lakeshore.

For motorists, hungry for hot food, residents recommend a drive a short distance south to Santiago's Mexican Restaurant in Porter. They recommend "Mama's Soup" and Santi's wine margaritas.

DUNES ACRES: Don't expect to find any commercial establishments in Dunes Acres. They are banned, for it is strictly a residential community, an exclusive town of 300 residents where uninvited visitors are not welcome.

The town was formed in the early 1920s by a group of Gary businessmen who leased 582 acres, which included some of the highest dunes in the area.

PORT OF INDIANA: Off U.S. 12 on Ind. 249 at Burns Harbor is the giant Port of Indiana, Indiana's first maritime center preceding those at Jeffersonville and Mount Vernon. The man-made facility opened northern Indiana to world trade via the St. Lawrence Seaway.

To the east is Bethlehem Steel, to the west Midwest Steel. Nearby are the multi-million dollar Cargill Inc. facilities which process more than 40 million bushels of grain a year. Not far away is the Union Carbide plant.

It is obvious the port has changed the face of the area and created new accesses to markets for industry.

Not all ventures are successful, however. The Bailly plant, a nuclear electric generating station started by the Northern Indiana Public Service Commission in 1970 was abandoned in 1981, the victim of public complaints and unexpected cost overruns.

OGDEN DUNES: Call this community on the lake luxurious, exclusive, special. It is a place for 1,500 residents to live without commercial distractions. There are no stores, no retail outlets.

As at Dunes Acres, guards prevent uninvited guests from entering the community. Streets are winding, homes are spacious, lots are large, and it is obvious this is a place to enjoy privacy in affluent surroundings.

No place, not even a paradise on the lake, is without problems. A sign at the guard house, posted by a grieving pet owner, reveals, "Calico Cat Lost."

* * *

We are entering Indiana's industrial northeast. A whiskey brown smog hangs over the area as we approach Lake County.

LAKE COUNTY

Established in 1836 and named for the lake to its north. Population 525,000, second largest in state behind Marion County. Most of lake area is heavily industrialized but terrain varies from sand dunes to rolling prairies. Western border is 34 miles long.

MILLER

A Part Of Gary

Miller, incorporated as a town in the early 1900s but annexed to Gary in 1918, remains a resort area with beach front homes amid the sand dunes.

It was here in the early 1900s that fishermen departed to salvage ice from the lake in winter and store it for use when the weather warmed.

The town has renovated its brick town hall, which originally was an electric substation and later a fire station.

Not far away is Marquette Park, a popular swimming beach. It was the spot from where French aviation pioneer Octave Chanute made the world's first successful heavier-than-air flight in a glider.

GARY

Miles of Steel

Motorists who pass through Gary on I-90 miss some of its attractions on the lake.

Visitors can learn about the area's ecosystem through exhibits at the Paul H. Douglas Environmental Center on Lake Street.

Gary is expecting a rebirth with the arrival of its riverboat casino and new entertainment complexes. Tourism officials advise travelers seeking more information to call a City of Gary Special Events number.

We leave U.S. 12 and take I-90, the Indiana toll road, past the Gary works of the USX (U.S. Steel Corporation). Steel mills — long buildings extending the length of several football fields — stretch more than four miles along the interstate.

The sky is overcast, penetrated only by a bright sun. The smell of molten steel and the sulphuric odor of oil refineries penetrate the nostrils.

It is a malodorous scent that will remain as we continue west and north through the heavily industrialized cities of Hammond, East Chicago and Whiting.

* * *

It is difficult to tell where one city begins, another starts, each tied together in an industrial metropolis of steel mills, refineries and factories.

Each city, built in the shadows of heavy industrial plants and refineries, has its own attractions beyond its industrial might. Each has its own heritage, each is home to the people who live here, many, perhaps, more comfortable among the population density than in the open spaces further south in Lake County.

Residents in the area have long felt more attuned to Chicago than to the rest of Indiana. Streets in Hammond, Whiting and East Chicago retain the Chicago numbering system.

State legislators from the area often complain that the Gary-East Chicago-Hammond complex is unappreciated by downstate Hoosiers. In the 1930s, legislators from the area introduced a bill to establish Lake County as the 49th state, but the measure failed after passing the second reading.

All the towns in the industrial arc around the lake retain the ethnic influence of groups who came to the area in the early 1900s when unskilled jobs were plentiful. One census showed 53 percent foreign born in East Chicago, 49 percent in Gary, 43 percent in Whiting and 26 percent in Hammond. The area became the homes of thousands of Poles, Czecks, Slovaks, Hungarians, Serbs, Croatians, Slovenes, Romanians, Greeks, Russians and Italians.

Blacks from the south were recruited to work at the steel mills around 1920 when European immigration was limited. Mexicans began arriving about the same time.

EAST CHICAGO
Shadows Of Steel

East Chicago has kept its own identity amid the congestion of the Calumet metroplex. It boasts of a rich 100-year history of ethnic diversity and cultural heritage, which is evidenced by its residential neighborhoods.

The Robert Pastrick Marina, which city promoters call "Northwest Indiana's jewel on the lake," is the shadows of a steel plant. It is a facility that brings relaxation and recreation to a work environment.

The Sails Restaurant at the marina is said to offer "elegant dining with a romantic view of the harbor." Promoters say its Sunday brunches have attracted visitors from throughout the Midwest.

INDIANA HARBOR
Company Town

Not far away is Indiana Harbor, a town that developed near the lake as a settlement for workers at Inland Steel.

It kept its own identity after becoming a part of East Chicago and now is a heavily-Hispanic community although other ethnic groups remain.

WHITING
Oil City

One of the smaller cities in the Calumet area, Whiting, with a population of 5,200, calls itself "the Little City on the Lake." Its Whihala Beach, a nice park area on the lake, is crowded on this late spring day.

Not far away, the Amoco Oil Company refineries are in operation as they have been since 1899, processing crude oil on 235 acres that once were dunes and marshland.

No one escapes the foul-smelling crude, high in sulphur content. Residents learn to live with it. Amoco spent $55 million to reduce pollution in 1992 and — despite the odor that still remains — promises to continue to do its best to keep pollution to a minimum.

Despite the odor, the area refineries are a source of civic pride to residents and the Whiting High School (enrollment 290) athletic teams are called the Oilers.

It is in Whiting where a marker on the Lake Michigan Shore establishes Indiana's northwestern corner. From there the western border line continues due south for 135 miles to the Wabash River.

HAMMOND

Fine Dining

This is an area noted for its fine dining and Hammond has some of the best, one of those places is Phil Smidt's 85-year-old restaurant which is noted for its frog legs and perch. The El Taco Real features authentic Mexican food.

Hammond, a city of 85,000 residents, has avoided some of the crime that has hurt Gary's image.

Among the city's attractions is the Hammond Civic Center and its 5,700-seat auditorium. The facility was built in the 1930s by the Works Progress Administration.

MUNSTER

Garden Stop

Munster is a far different place than it was in the mid-1800s when it was founded by Dutch immigrants whose truck farms produced vegetables for the Chicago market.

The farms are gone and Munster, just south of Hammond on U.S. 41, has become a suburban city of 20,000, growing rapidly in the decades since the mid-1900s.

Residents recommend a stop at the Carmelite Shrines where the monastery gardens are filled with unusual trees and shrubs, the indoor memorials being accentuated with imported crystals and colorful rocks.

HIGHLAND

The Way Things Were

The Highway of Flags Memorial is at the southeast corner of U.S. 41 and Ridge Road in Highland. Dedicated in 1975, it is a national shrine honoring the American flag as well as servicemen and women of all wars and conflicts.

To the south on U.S. 41 is the Miner-Dunn restaurant, home, a sign says, of the "prodigious tenderloin." It is not an idle boast as evidenced by the locals who have ordered it. The sandwich is excellent as could be expected in a place that has survived since 1932 when two men opened it despite the Great Depression.

* * *

Amidst the urban sprawl is Hoosier Prairie, another of Indiana's surprises, which is a look back at the land as settlers saw it when they arrived.

Hoosier Prairie is a short distance east of U.S. 41 on the south side of Main Street — the dividing line between Highland and Schererville. About 335 acres of virgin land have been restored as a state nature preserve and national landmark. It is here that visitors can see how the area looked before civilization changed what nature had created.

* * *

U.S. 41 is heavily commercialized and a haze remains over the area, a bright sun unable to penetrate the overcast.

SCHERERVILLE

Boom Town

This is another Calumet suburb that has grown into a populated region in the last few years, becoming a far different place than it was when it was a crossroads of Indian trails. From 1970 to 1990, Schererville's population rose from 3,663 to 19,926. Chances are it will be well into the 20,000s by the next count in 2000.

Despite its recent growth, it is older than many nearby towns, having been founded in 1866.

ST. JOHN

Changing Times

Lake Central High School on U.S. 41 in St. John reflects the big shift of population to the south central suburbs of Lake County. The high school, less than 30 years old (its 1967 graduating class being its first), now is among the largest in the state with 2,500 students.

The school absorbed Dyer and takes in students from St. John and Schererville.

St. John was one of the earliest settlements in the county, having been founded in 1837. Within a few years it had the largest German Catholic population in Lake County.

* * *

U.S. 41 from Hammond to St. John has been a continuous commercial highway, businesses lining each side of the road for miles.

* * *

The congestion begins to ease to the south and we leave U.S. 41 and drive west toward the Illinois border on 93rd Avenue. New housing developments, the homes huge, rise on the rolling terrain.

At Sheffield Avenue we turn south past additional subdivisions where houses are growing on land once reserved for crops.

KREITZBURG

The Future Is Near

If people come, commerce is certain to follow. At Sheffield Avenue and 101st Avenue near Kreitzburg, a sign at an open field promises: "Shopping Center — Office and Retail Space Available."

Until now, Kreitzburg, founded in 1880, has never been much of a town. Oh, it had a blacksmith shop, tavern and general store as did most neighborhood communities. All are gone now, so have any businesses.

Only a few modest houses remain. But that is about to change. It is likely the community just east of the Illinois border will be surrounded by new development, the proposed shopping center planned nearby an indication of things to come.

* * *

South of Kreitzburg, the land flattens, the fields become larger, the smog disappears and the air is free from the essence of sulphur. This is the Indiana most Hoosiers know.

An indication of stability in an area of change is a place identified as "Piepho Homestead Farm — 1852" near the intersection of 109th and Calumet Avenue. Not far away is the Zion United Church of Christ, "standing silent watch over the prairie," its welcome sign says.

The land becomes rolling as State Line Road goes south past a few suburban homes. The farms are larger. The air is clear and in the smogless view to the east a ridge of trees rises above the prairie.

BRUNSWICK

A Friendly Tavern

The past and the future meet at Brunswick, a mile from the state line.

Germans settled here in 1858 and named the place for the state and city they had left behind in Europe. It remained a farm town for 130 years before new residents found the housing development on the north side and decided Brunswick was a good place for the good life.

Brunswick until about 1990 was the home of the Perfection Musical String Company. The factory achieved international recognition for the quality of its violin, viola, cello and bass viol strings. It is said workers spun silver or aluminum casings around animal intestine cores with winding machines built on the premises.

Gone, too, is a garage that indicates it may have once been an auto dealership, a Hudson emblem hanging at the gable of the tile building. What once was a general store is now a residence.

But Reichert's Tavern is open, thriving, in fact, as Brunswick's only commercial enterprise and serving beer, wine, sandwiches . . . and endless conversation. All the stools and some of the tables are occupied in mid-afternoon on a Monday in June.

Bartender Tammy Briton says the size of the crowd isn't unusual. "Oh, Monday is a slow day. We're busier than this on other afternoons."

Most of the customers are regulars, Tammy says. "It's a friendly nice crowd, quiet, not the kind that creates problems." It is a fun group, too, the kind that can appreciate a sign over the beer coolers: "Men: No shirt, no service. Women: No shirt, free drinks."

Reichert's is said to be the oldest tavern operating under its original name in Lake County. The bar and fixtures may be as old as the tavern, which opened in 1915.

Newspapers stories, the pages yellowing, tell about the town and the bar. One puts the population of Brunswick at 75 residents. That was before the housing boom reached town. Dozens of new expensive homes, built on sizable lots, have been built in the last five years, probably tripling the size of Brunswick.

Land that once produced 150-bushel-per-acre corn crops now grow houses, two to the acre.

* * *

Just south of Brunswick on Calumet Avenue are two identical 90-year-old round barns behind a farm house that also has a circular shape. The barns do not appear to be in use.

Identical round barns near "round" house

A rounded shape farm house near Brunswick

KLAASVILLE

Buried By Time

We return to State Line Road and find the community of Klaasville at Sheffield Avenue and 145th Avenue.

It was a town founded in 1850 by a man named H. Klaas. Most of its history appears to be buried in St. Anthony's Cemetery, which is surrounded by a woven wire fence.

Only three or four houses and a few farms make up the community today. That could change if the constant tide of suburban movement continues to sprawl south.

* * *

We continue south, past farm land, noticing the change from the Calumet area a few miles to the north. Silos have replaced smokestacks. The only reminders of industrialized Indiana are the giant transmission lines that cross the prairie.

SCHNEIDER

A man walking on the street, unaccustomed to being greeted first, reluctantly returns our wave as we enter Schneider off U.S. 41.

It is a farm community along U.S. 41 on the north side of the Kankakee River, which separates Lake from Newton County to the south. Populated towns are to the north, but Schneider, population 425, has its own library, post office and a tavern called "Jack's or Better." The Lions Club Park includes a shelter house and basketball court.

West of Schneider is the LaSalle state fish and wildlife area, which extends on both sides of the Kankakee to the Illinois line. Its 3,648 acres is home to bluegill, bass, catfish, rough fish and walleye as well as deer, dove, waterfowl, squirrel and woodcock in the river and bayous.

* * *

We have completed our exploration of the Lake County border. It has been a study in contrasts.

On The West

NEWTON COUNTY

Named for Sgt. John Newton, a Revolutionary War hero. Established as the last county in Indiana in 1859. Rural area with huge farms and rich land except for swampy areas, most of which have been drained. Population 15,000.

SUMAVA RESORTS

A Planned Community

Sumava Resorts is a town that never quite lived up to the dreams of its developers back in the pre-depression era. No matter! It is still home to a few hundred residents who enjoy life here on the south side of the Kankakee.

Real estate developers from Chicago bought the land in 1927, platted lots and enticed would-be buyers with free train rides from the Windy City to what was promoted as "the picturesque winding Kankakee River."

The curious came by the hundreds, riding on crowded excursion trains from Chicago, carrying picnic lunches for a day's relaxation mixed with the salesmanship of promoters.

Some visitors, awed by the serenity and scenery in contrast to the city, bought lots and built houses. In the beginning, the residences were summer cottages where people came for the weekend, using the river for recreation.

More permanent houses were built later and some older people stayed, making Sumava Resorts a year-round community.

Trains no longer bring passengers to Sumava, which is east of U.S. 41. Nor do many cars arrive either for most motorists bypass the community. Those who do stop will find friendly folks like Venus and James Lukes.

We meet Mrs. Lukes at the Sumava Post Office, where she once was postmaster. She and Jim also ran Lukes Restaurant next door until their son, Thomas, took over the operation. The restaurant, which has been in the Lukes family for more than 55 years, boasts of "quality food at reasonable prices." It is worth a stop for weekend travelers on U.S. 41 who want pleasant dining amid history.

"My husband's parents bought this building which was a community hall, moved it to this location and opened the restaurant in 1940," Mrs. Lukes explains.

The restaurant walls are lined with pictures of the Sumava of 1930 as well as an original plat map showing how the community was laid out. There also are photographs of the great waters of 1950 when the Kankakee flooded and inundated the area, a disaster that did not drive out hardy folks like the Lukes.

Except for two restaurants (the Sumava Inn being the other) there are no commercial enterprises in Sumava Resorts. The convenience store and bakery, which were in the post office building, closed when Mrs. Lukes retired in 1989 after a 32-year career as town postmaster.

The post office, where residents pick up their mail from boxes, remains open.

* * *

We drive south through Lake Village, a town of 650 residents on the east side of U.S. 41. An industrial park offers sites for new industry in a rural setting away from the congestion to the north.

South of Lake Village the richness of Newton County is evident as unfenced land begins to extend to the horizons. The significance of agriculture in Indiana is again obvious. It is a sharp contrast to the industrial might of the Calumet area.

Houses are few, at times three to four miles apart. The farms are huge, the fields almost endless, some that seem as large as some Third World nations.

Off to the right is North Newton High School, a consolidation of Morocco and Mt. Ayr. Despite the merger, the high school has but 450 students, reflecting the sparseness of the population in the rural farm land.

* * *

Life appears to be good in this land that is free on this day of smog and clouds. Crime would appear to be a stranger. We are surprised, however, when we reach Enos, a small farm center, and see an office marked "Marijuana Eradication." The weed grows wild in the area and police agencies take pains each year to destroy the crop before it is harvested by those who would turn it into cash.

* * *

Southwest of Enos on the Illinois border is the Willow Slough state fish and wildlife area, a 9,938-acre marshland which offers fishing opportunities for bluegill, catfish and pike fishing in Purphey Lake. Hunters, in season, can search out deer, dove, upland game, squirrel, water fowl and woodcock. Camping and picnicking are available.

* * *

Grain elevators, that once were landmarks for rural towns, now dot the prairie landscape, towering over farmsteads instead of communities. There are no housing developments, no suburban sprawl. This is prime farm land, so rich and productive it is best that bulldozers and contractors look elsewhere for development.

MOROCCO
Small But Busy

One of the few commercial centers in Newton County, Morocco is proud of its hospitality and its member of the Baseball Hall of Fame.

Signs at the entrance to town note it was the home of Edgar "Sam" Rice, a 20-year American League outfielder (1915-1934 — batting average .322) who was inducted into the Hall of Fame in 1966.

Visitors also are greeted with "Welcome to Morocco — Home of Hoosier Hospitality" signs and promotions for "Morocco Fun Days," which are the third weekend each June.

In the center of town are small businesses, a pharmacy, license branch, newspaper office, insurance agency, bank branches and farm stores.

The quiet town of 1,000 residents appears to be the center of activity for the northern half of the county.

ADE

The Town, The Man

A grain elevator and farm center are still in operation in Ade, a community of 20 or so homes west of U.S. 41 at Roads 275 West and 900 South.

Swans have taken up residence for the summer on a pond at one of the homes in town. This is Ade Country, as in George Ade, (1866-1944), the noted playwright, humorist, author and newspaper columnist who was born in nearby Kentland.

East of Ade on Ind. 16 is Brook, a farm town with a population of 950 that was home to Ade, who once had three plays running at the same time on Broadway.

* * *

We drive a mile west of U.S. 41 on Road 1150 South to a historical marker near Road 300 West. A plaque on a boulder notes the site of the first church in Newton County, leaving visitors to reflect on what the prairie was like when the Rev. Frederick Kenoyer delivered his first sermon in those pioneer days of 1839.

Not far away we see a few cattle, the first livestock we have seen since we left LaPorte County. There were none of course in the urbanized northwest, none on the vast grain farms along the Illinois border to the north.

* * *

We cross the Iroquois River, which flows 50 miles west into Illinois from its origin in Jasper County near Kentland.

East off U.S. 41 is South Newton High School, a consolidation of Kentland, Brook, Goodland and Raub with an enrollment of 330 students in four grades.

KENTLAND

Farm And Industry

Vast farms and small factories converge in Kentland, a town which notes it is "where agriculture and industry meet."

The business center of southern Newton County, it is one of the states smallest county seats, home to 1,800 residents, many of whom are retired farmers.

It is here that U.S. 24, on its way west into Illinois, intersects with U.S. 41.

The Nu-Joy Restaurant is in the Alexander Kent mansion, but it — to our loss — is not open on Mondays. Kent founded the town in 1860 and his home is one of the largest in the community. There are two other family restaurants. One is Hudgen's, where everyone seems to know everyone else, if not he or she soon will. No one will remain a stranger long. It is at Hudgen's where farmers exchange friendly banter over breakfast.

Kentland is the home of Funk & Sons seed corn company, which is appropriate for this is the heart of grain country.

* * *

We take U.S. 24 toward the state line, then go south on Ind. 71 through what once was vast prairie land. Farms are huge and numerous. Giant storage bins and other outbuildings make what few homesteads there are seem as big as some towns.

Ind. 71 is narrow but smooth. A male pheasant shuffles away from the pavement into a cornfield. The land is flat, the soil black and rich. Pine trees line homes to the north and west, breaks against frigid winter winds that can lash unrelentlessly at times. This, however, is not one of those times. The air is warm and still for it is planting season and the days are long and enjoyable.

BENTON COUNTY

Created in 1840 and named for U.S. Sen. Thomas Hart Benton. Population 10,500, with no congested areas. County seat is at Fowler. One of state's most important farm counties, with almost its entire acreage devoted to agriculture.

RAUB

Keeping Posted

Small town Hoosiers do not forget those who fought to keep them safe. The folks in Raub haven't. A Veterans' Memorial — in the town park amid apple trees — notes the names of men from the area who served in World War I, World War II, Korea, Vietnam and Operation Desert Storm.

Raub is small, just south of the Newton County line, and like most farm communities, its past is bigger than its present.

At the east side of town, a dog stands watch over the post office, ZIP Code 47976, located in a part of what once was the two-story brick Raub School, officially "York Township School" built in 1915.

Students in town no longer are the Raub Hornets or the Raub Ramblers as they once were. They now cross the county line to attend South Newton, where the athletic teams are known as the Rebels.

Except for the Demeter Farm Center there are no businesses, no stores. A fast food restaurant or a convenience store is miles away.

A sign at a town well says, "For fire use only. Non-drinkable. Keep this area clear."

The Raub United Methodist Church, a frame building painted white, appears to be the center of activity, its sign proclaiming, "A family in Christ serving the people of our community and the world."

* * *

The endless prairie continues as we head south from Raub on Ind. 71 along the Illinois state line. Homes are two, sometimes three, miles apart. The houses are large, well cared for, mostly two stories except for a few newer ranch style homes. Almost all are painted white and are well maintained.

Fields stretch for a mile or more along the endless, unbroken horizon, the farms appearing as large as townships. It is obvious what once were small operations now are part of giant enterprises, the farms growing larger as the number of farmers become fewer.

Another pheasant runs from the road into a field. We are alone in the isolation. There is little traffic and we drive for two, sometimes three, miles without seeing another car.

* * *

Off to the east, south of Ind. 18, a giant grain elevator rises 150 feet or more above the horizon. It, like dozens of others in this area of the state, is a beacon for the lost for reference points are few in the vast expanse.

The elevator leads to Free, a community of three farmsteads near a massive grain operation next to the railroad. It is an example of the importance of agribusiness to the county and to the state.

FREELAND PARK

No Rockets Glare

Off Ind. 18 is Freeland Park, another town that appears lost in time. Like hundreds of other Hoosier towns, Freeland Park lost much of its identity when its school closed and students moved to consolidated Benton Central.

No matter how much they try, the support for the bigger school is not as avid as it was for the Rockets teams which gave Freeland Park a sense of purpose.

Not many houses remain. Most of those that do ring the town park. A playhouse on stilts and an above ground swimming pool give evidence Freeland Park is a family town.

No stores remain. The nearest fast food restaurant is miles away.

DUNNINGTON

A Church Town

The land remains fertile south of Freeland Park, the fields again endless, the view unobstructed. A farmer in a pickup truck waves a greeting as we meet on Ind. 71.

Up ahead, a church spire, visible for miles, rises above St. Mary's Catholic Church in the community of Dunnington. The brick church, built in 1950, is an imposing structure, a dominant landmark in the open prairies that surround it.

Giant trees dominate the grounds around the church and rectory. A cemetery is across Ind. 71. A number of cars are parked at the church on a Tuesday morning, an indication it is a community center for the farm families that live in the area.

A half dozen houses are near the church. What once was a store is closed, a soft drink vending machine and an ice machine left out front. Two rusting thermometers remain tacked on the outside wall.

* * *

Dunnington has the church; Dunn, to the east, has the railroad and the farm center. A storage bin towers over six silos at the Demeter Inc. grain storage operation.

Nearby farms have their own grain storage facilities and it appears a Harvestore salesman may have made a fortune peddling the blue silos that dot the landscape.

* * *

Ind. 71 ends, at least for a few miles, at east-west Ind. 352, which leads toward the community of Ambia. For the first time in 100 miles, roadside trees block our view of the horizon.

AMBIA

Community Pride

Community pride remains in Ambia, although time and conditions have changed and the town no longer is as busy as it once was.

Streets are named, the Christian and Methodist Churches are well maintained. The site of the old Ambia School has been turned into a memorial park by the Ambia Alumni Association. A brick wall 8 feet high is marked: "Memorial — Ambia High School, 1899 - 1968. Dedicated June 24, 1989, by the Ambia Alumni Association."

Consolidation has not detracted from the pride former students have in their school and its Wildcat teams.

The railroad still runs through town, but the depot is abandoned as is the grain elevator, grocery and Ambia State Bank. A service station no longer is in business. There is no convenience store, no restaurant, only a couple of commercial businesses. What once was a two-story brick business center is vacant, except for pigeons.

The newest buildings in town are the post office and the Hickory Grove Township Fire Department.

A resident stops on his way to the post office to talk about the town. "The loss of the school hurt Ambia," he explains. "When the school closed, the town lost its identity, its togetherness.

"A few people have tried to operate groceries and gas stations, but they couldn't make a go of it. Stores in towns this size can't compete against the Wal-Marts and superstores. Now we have to do most of our shopping in Lafayette or go across the Illinois line and shop at Hoopeston or Danville."

He explains the name Ambia. "It was founded in 1875 by a man named Ezekel Talbot who named it after his daughter, Ambia."

HANDY

The Name Remains

We drive east toward Boswell, the nearest town with a restaurant and public restroom.

On the way is a place marked on a Benton County map as "Handy." Handy it turns out is about the size of its name which is on a white on blue sign tacked to an abandoned two-story brick railroad depot.

Chances are this was a "Handy" place for farmers back before cars and trucks allowed them to leave the area to shop . . . and before on-farm granaries eliminated the need for an elevator at every railroad stop.

TALBOT
Population 10

A mile or so away is the farm community of Talbot, where two railroads cross.

A sign explains the town was named after Ambia's founder Ezekel Talbot, then chief engineer of the LM & B Railroad. Another sign notes, "Talbot — Population 10."

A store noting "Keadle Block — July 26, 1898" — is abandoned. A cat now uses the building as its private abode, sneaking through a hole at the bottom of the door.

BOSWELL
The Farmers Table

Boswell turns out to be a busy place for a town of 750 residents. Its banks, food market, restaurants and stores serve a wide area of southwestern Benton County, from U.S. 41 west to the Illinois line.

The Farmers Table restaurant is busy at mid-morning, a friendly place where farmers gather to discuss the weather, grain prices and commodity markets.

One of them walks out into the parking lot and points to an impressive but vacant three-story brick house. "It had the first indoor plumbing in Boswell," he explains. "A tank in the back allowed water to flow by gravity into the house."

The house is now a one-time mansion in search of a caretaker.

WARREN COUNTY

The Wabash River flows southwest across the southern border, shaping the county into a triangle. Created in 1827, the county was named for Gen. Joseph Warren, a commander at Bunker Hill. Population 8,200. County seat at Williamsport.

TAB

Place In The Sun

We drive south from Ambia along the state line, crossing from Benton to Warren County, then take a crushed stone road to the community of Tab. A trail of dust follows.

The only identification is a "Tab" sign on a pole next to the railroad tracks, a marker which once let train engineers know their location.

An old but well-maintained farm house, big enough for a hotel, is at the west edge of town. There are few houses, but streets are named. An American flag flies at one home. Clothes dry in the sun on a line at another house.

It is another community with a high-rise grain elevator, which towers above five other silos.

State lines are imaginary boundaries here where residents are as attuned to Illinois as Indiana and most newspaper tubes are marked *Danville Sun-Commercial*.

*   *   *

It is summer and there are no surprise visitors at rural homes in this part of the county. The dust from the crushed stone roads form clouds behind cars, betraying any attempt to make unannounced visits.

We continue south on another dusty crushed stone road, then drive east on County Road 300 North to Stewart, a place that also owes its history to the railroad and the farms that surround it.

PENCE

Crossroads Town

The community of Pence, a ghost of its past, is west of Stewart on County Road 300 North.

Four store fronts in a two-story brick building are closed, littered inside with items no longer useful. The upstairs windows are boarded over, except for one section where pigeons have taken up residence.

The only business is a seed company. What once was a garage is closed. A long Quonset-type building at the edge of town is vacant, except for a few bushels of shelled corn.

Most homes, including manufactured houses, have well-tended gardens.

HEDRICK

"Inner Peace"

South of Pence a small sign atop a speed limit marker informs motorists they are in Hedrick, a residential community amid cornfields.

American flags fly over small homes, proving patriotism knows no economic status. Homes are modest, but well maintained. Streets are named.

The Hedrick Assembly of God Church is next to the Church of God, Abrahamic Faith, where a sign advises, "A quiet time with God each day will produce an inner peace."

There are no retail businesses, just a farm center at the east edge of town.

* * *

A short distance east of Hedrick is another old railroad town, identified as Sloan by the white on blue railroad sign tacked to a post.

Occupants of a double-wide manufactured home with an above ground swimming pool are the only residents. An abandoned store and three grain storage silos stand as ghosts of the past.

* * *

We have driven 100 miles or so through corn and soybean country, past farms, which with one exception, are without livestock. The terrain is becoming rolling, the fields smaller as we continue south. A field of wheat, the first we have seen along the Illinois border, awaits the combine south of Sloan.

MARSHFIELD

A Corvette Town

We cross Ind. 28 and find the community of Marshfield on County Road 450 North at the Norfolk & Western Railroad.

A detailed sign notes, "Marshfield — founded in 1857 during early railroad boom. Named for the Massachusetts home of Daniel Webster, a political leader, administrator and diplomat. Established as a post office April 6, 1857."

The Marshfield grain elevator, a division of the Stewart Grain Company, is in operation. Freight cars line the railroad siding.

Two tractors, only one car, wait at a crossing while a train rumbles through town, an indication of the impact of farming in the area.

An auto body shop specializes in Corvette repairs for rural folks have as much interest in sports cars as urbanites.

JOHNSONVILLE

"Fear Not"

Johnsonville is a curve in the road over the Norfolk & Western, which cuts diagonally from southwest to northeast.

The road, now paved, curves at the railroad crossing and motorists are grateful for the barricades that drop when fast moving trains pass.

Johnsonville has a church, three houses beside the railroad and no stores or businesses. A sign on a woven wire fence reads: "Johnsonville, founded in 1876."

The Williams Chapel Community Church bulletin board cites a Scripture from Luke: "Fear not little flock, for it is your Father's good pleasure to give you the kingdom."

A row of hollyhocks lines the north side of the church property, a flower seldom seen in the late 1990s.

* * *

We continue south from Johnsonville on the blacktop Warren County road. The terrain changes from flat to rolling, with some wooded areas. Fields are not as large as they were to the north.

Two women, each with small children, have pulled off the side of the road to — in the parlance of the 1990s — interact. Neighbors are few and far between so it is good to exchange news.

We reach County Road 650 south and go west toward the border and drive to State Line City.

STATE LINE CITY
A Twin Town

State Line City is part of two cities astraddle the Indiana-Illinois Line. State Line is in Indiana, Illiana is on the Illinois side. One post office, State Line, serves both towns.

The flat prairie stretches in all directions from State Line, home to a few hundred people, including, Milton Anderson.

Anderson, a retiree who is working in his yard on this spring morning, doesn't mind our intrusion. He warns, however, that the moisture from his lush lawn grass may soak into our shoes.

"Lived here quite a while," he says. "It's a nice, quiet town." He adds, quickly, "Sometimes, that is. Once in a while it gets kinda loud, like all the rest of the towns."

If there are differences between Hoosiers and Illini, Anderson hasn't detected them. "We're all the same," he says.

"People don't change much," he adds, "but towns do. State Line, like all other small places, is different than it once was. We used to have a couple of garages, two or three filling stations, a bank.

"We had a depot where passenger trains stopped. The railroad is still here, but now freight trains stop only for the grain elevator. All the stores are gone, so are the restaurants. Now we go west to Danville (Ill.) or east to Covington, both of which are about 10 miles away, to shop."

A Dr. Pepper machine appears to be the only retail outlet in town.

The park in the center of State Line is well maintained. Despite the decline in retail business, the town appears to be alive and well and a few folks have chosen to build new homes.

We drive out of town, easing past a 16-row corn planter which takes up most of a State Line Street.

* * *

At a turn in the road southeast of State Line, a rusted marker in the yard of a farm home notes the Harrison Trail:

"In the yard of this home is visible the trail followed by the heavy wagons of the Army under Gen. Harrison (William Henry) passing here on the way to Tippecanoe, November 3, 1811."

Gopher Hill No. 3, a historic school which is a landmark of the past, is now a residence at County Road 850 South and 900 West. Just to the south is the Gopher Hill Cemetery.

VERMILLION COUNTY

Sometimes called Indiana's shoestring county because of its shape. It averages 7 miles in width and stretches 37 miles along the Illinois border. Founded in 1824 and named for the Vermillion River. Population 17,000. County seat is at Newport, population 650.

———

We reach Vermillion County, which is just two miles wide at this point, and drive south across U.S. 36 toward Rileysburg, a community of a dozen homes.

A Massey-Ferguson farm implement dealership appears to be the only business in town. What looks to have been a school is deteriorating. A junk yard is behind it, a mobile home to its side.

* * *

The community of Gessie is a mile south and a mile east. The Gessie United Methodist Church reminds visitors: "God wants to travel with us on our way." It is an appropriate message for those touring this area of the state.

The Seaboard System railroad runs through town, past the grain elevator. The post office no longer is in operation although there are more homes than some communities which have maintained theirs.

EUGENE

A Span Of Time

We have encountered few surprises on this leg of the trip for most of the stops have been at tiny towns identified by their grain operations.

Eugene, on the banks of Big Vermillion River a few miles south of Gessie, is an exception. A covered bridge, saved from extinction by members of Delta Theta Tau in 1963, spans the river as it has since it was built by J.J. Daniels in 1873.

Unused 120-year-old covered bridge at Eugene

Across the new bridge is the Covered Bridge Restaurant, a popular eating place worth a stop. Also of note is the Eugene Methodist Church built in 1858, its four square columns giving it an impressive front. The message on the information board out front offers a thought for the week: "More people get run down by gossip than by cars."

Across the street from the church is an old school with a paved basketball court in need of repair. A message there warns, "Not responsible for accidents. The trustee."

The Roy and Mary Clark Building, which appears to have been a store, is closed. A soft drink vending machine remains out front.

Eugene is unincorporated, has no post office and no stores other than the restaurant, a big change from the days when the town had a grist mill on the river from where it shipped grain and pork to New Orleans.

It was Eugene where Alice Craig Fuller wrote *Lantern Gleams of Old Eugene* and other poems.

CAYUGA

Community Calendar

A mile or so southeast of Eugene is Cayuga, a small town that has survived, perhaps prospered, despite changing times and the loss of its high school.

It is home to 1,100 residents, all of whom live within walking distance of stores and businesses, the post office, taverns, an auto dealership, health center, drug store, the Town Hall, the fire department, the community park, the church of their choice, and, in times of sorrow, the funeral home.

It is small town Indiana. A man runs a lawn mower down the street, others are on their morning walks. A recycling center is open.

It is almost noon, but the Logan 105 Restaurant is still serving breakfast and the weekly news. "The Herald News," an eight-page tabloid "serving Northern Vermillion County," is a bulletin board of sorts for the residents of Cayuga. It lists dates and times of community meetings, provides information from the county extension service, and reports personal items such as: "Paul and Georgia Crowder of Arizona have arrived in Cayuga for the summer months."

Not all strangers are welcome in Cayuga. In a classified notice, the Marcinko Land Company warns that its farm in Vermillion Township is closed to all hunting. "This includes mushroom, ginseng, deer, or any other type of hunting. All trespassers will be prosecuted."

High school students, who once were the Cayuga Indians, now attend nearby North Vermillion, a consolidation where athletes are called Falcons.

* * *

An old concrete road leads southwest out of Cayuga, past some nice country homes. The terrain turns rolling, even hilly for a time southwest of Cayuga. Wild flowers are in bloom on the banks of the road. The dogwood have painted the awakening hills with coats of white.

Farms remain large despite the rolling fields that line the country roads. The upright concrete sides of narrow bridges are painted fluorescent as warning to motorists.

Towering steel structures, skeletons with arms, grasp transmission lines that carry electricity across the country.

We continue south, generally following the Little Vermillion River. The road winds as if laid out by a scared snake and a sign warns of "dangerous curves ahead."

A quail at the side of the road waits until the last second to fly off as a car approaches. The road follows a ridge, then declines a hill past graffiti-marred signs until it reaches the river.

The road passes the Hopewell Friends Church, which is across from the sizable Ellis Polled Hereford farm, en route to a place on the map identified as Quaker.

Quaker, a border community two miles west of Ind. 71, is more of a farm center than a town. It is here where the Quaker Division of the Kentland Elevator — "serving the heart of the cornbelt" — is located. Nearby is a fertilizer and chemical company outlet.

* * *

The terrain changes abruptly south of Quaker as we skirt the state line. Hills level off, the fields again are flat, the soil rich dark loam. Houses are few and far between, some a mile or so apart.

Again the view is unobstructed, the water towers at rural towns visible for miles.

A hand pump remains out front of a modern home, a reminder of the past when homes had no running water or plumbing.

We follow the state line south to Dana, another farm center and the home of Ernie Pyle.

DANA
Pride In The Past

Current residents of Dana want visitors to know it was the home of the famed World War II correspondent. "Visit the Ernie Pyle State Memorial," a marker suggests.

Pyle's rural home, which was moved to town from its farm setting, is now a state historic site. The new Visitor's Center was dedicated on April 18, 1995, the 50th anniversary of Pyle's death from Japanese machine gun fire on Ie Shima. An estimated 3,000 visitors came to Dana for that dedication, evidence that Pyle had not been forgotten.

Visitors can reflect on the past at the museum. They can also look back in time at Our Town Sundries, also known as "Jackie's Tender Loving Care," a combination gift shop and restaurant.

The walls of the shop are lined with pictures of graduates of Dana High School, which no longer exist. High school students attend a consolidation called South Vermillion while grade school students attend Ernie Pyle Elementary south of Dana.

Residents appear to take as much pride in their homes as in their heritage. Homes are well-maintained, so are the town library and town hall.

Dana is landlocked in the center of the midwestern prairie, which makes the giant transmitting tower near town seem out of place. Five Coast Guard personnel are stationed in the little white building next to the tower, which transmits signals to ships on the Great Lakes.

* * *

A Vermillion County map pinpoints Randall near the state line. If Randall is still a town, it is well hidden for we do not locate it.

We drive the State Line south of U.S. 36, the road similar to a one-lane drive to a private home. A home is abandoned, a small operator giving up life on the farm, overtaken by a bigger operator in a business where only the large survive.

An old barn painted red is decorated with an I.U. emblem. Not far away a driveway to a farm home is lined with globe lights.

We return over county roads, through black, rich land, to Ind. 71 and a settlement identified as "Bono" by painted lettering on a rock.

Bono has eight or ten houses built around the Bono Methodist Church, established in 1851 when the area was new and pioneers were seeking better lives. A half-mile to the west on a small knoll is the Bono Cemetery which surrounds a small chapel on the grounds. The entry into the graveyard warns, "No vehicles allowed after dark."

* * *

Back on Ind. 71 we pass a Frito-Lay delivery driver whose stops are few and far between in this area where miles are many and stores are few.

We turn off Ind. 71. and take a rough road littered with chuckholes in search of asphalt, a virtual washboard. Our destination is Jonestown.

JONESTOWN

An Oasis No More

Empty buildings indicate Jonestown once was a larger place, a similar circumstance of dozens of other communities around the state.

American Legion Post 108 of St. Bernice is in a brick building, circa 1910, that once was the Hilt Township School. A shelter house is on the grounds. So is a pump, its handle wired, a reminder when students got their drinking water from wells.

There are few houses in Jonestown, but residences line a county road a mile west toward St. Bernice. The road passes the wrecked remains of St. Bernice High School which was ravaged by a tornado three decades ago and never rebuilt.

ST. BERNICE

Big On Bingo

St. Bernice, a coin toss from Illinois, had 950 residents at last count, but not much is happening in town on this day. It wasn't like that decades ago when Chicago, Milwaukee & St. Paul Railroad trains stopped as they skirted the west edge of Vermillion County.

A woman under a big straw hat mows the lawn from atop a riding tractor. She returns a wave. Most of the homes are modest, the streets out front surrendering to chuckholes which erase any desire for motorists to speed.

The library branch is closed, but is open on Saturday mornings, a sign says. The Volunteer Fire Department in one of the better buildings in town advertises its fund-raising bingo games, which may be St. Bernice's biggest social attraction.

The St. Bernice tavern has its front door open, awaiting Friday afternoon customers. A building that appears to have housed three or four stores is no longer in use, the years taking its toll.

A convenience store, with gas pumps, is at the south edge of town where the homes are newer. St. Bernice sportsmen's club is off the road south.

The road — and the terrain beyond — rises and falls south of St. Bernice on the way to Blanford.

BLANFORD

The Town Tavern

Marianne Hutson, wearing a white T shirt with blue "Ice Budweiser" lettering, is at work at Lance's Hut, a bar and restaurant.

She is part owner of the place and is not hesitant to talk with strangers. Neither is a customer, seated at the bar, drinking draft beer. Together they describe the Blanford of today and the Blanford of an earlier time when coal was king and the town was bigger.

The man at the bar, citing conversation with his grandmother, says, "Back in the '20s and '30s the town had 1,200 residents and no churches."

It was a town where first and second generations of Italians, Serbs and Slovaks came, seeking — and finding — work in the mines. Marianne's grandfather, a native of Czeckoslovakia, was one of them.

Marianne adds, "There were so many taverns there was no room for churches. There were five taverns, plus three bootleggers right near this main corner, probably as late as the 1950s. There also were four groceries."

Times have changed. Except for a car wash and the tavern, not much remains, only homes and the recreation area, which is maintained by the Vermillion County Park Board. The park is named for James Perona, a reflection of the Italian community once present in the town.

"When the post office closes at 5 p.m., this is the only place that's open," Marianne explains.

But the town of 500 still is a place filled with history . . . and lore. Consider this tale spun by the customer, after taking the first sip from his third draft beer:

"My grandmother and grandpa had a disagreement and grandma took the kids back in the woods behind the house. They'd been out there several days when grandpa finally got so mad he started moving the furniture outside.

"He was getting ready to burn it when Grandma stopped him. She had a machine gun which she propped on a fence post and started firing. The shots tore through the outhouse, ripped up the garden and shattered Grandpa's wooden leg.

"My grandmother used to tell that story. Grandpa never said much about it, though."

There are other stories to be told about Blanford, but it is time to leave.

It is a Friday and in a few hours weekend customers will begin arriving. Band music will drown out the story telling, but not the camaraderie of a tavern in a small town.

* * *

Ind. 71 ends at the south edge of Blanford, Ind. 163 leads to the state line, where a farm straddles the Indiana-Illinois State Line. We turn and head southeast on Ind. 163 through the community of Centenary, a roadside community of several homes along the state highway.

Spaghetti must be a popular item in these parts. The township fire department advertises, "All you can eat spaghetti dinner." A tavern in an old house offers, "All you can eat spaghetti. $4.50."

* * *

From Centenary, we take county roads south past a number of nice suburban homes for we are not far from Clinton, whose population of 5,000 makes it Vermillion County's largest city.

UNIVERSAL

Good Times Gone

The town of Universal is easy to spot, its water tower high on a hill overlooking the Brouvilletts Creek bottoms.

The town was featured on a public television program the previous night, but no one in Universal seems to have seen the show. It is news to them.

A small store, about the size of a one-car garage, at the east edge of town offers "quick snacks and pop." The owner, who declines to identify himself, says he is a stranger in Universal. "Moved here from Arkansas to work at the Peabody Coal mine, which is now closed, so I don't know the town as well as some other folks."

He suggests we talk with Louie Secondino, who is 98. Secondino gives up a few minutes of the O.J. Simpson trial to talk. He may be two years short of a century, but he hears well, speaks easily and comprehends our interest.

He came to town in 1912, moving with his family from Cartis, Ill., a town that no longer exists. "My dad, who was from Italy, worked in coal mines and so did my brother, John. I worked in a clothing store in Cardis, then ran a grocery in Universal from 1914 until 1949 when it burned."

"Now there are no stores left in Universal, except that little place across the way where you stopped. The town has changed a lot, of course. We had some good times when I came here and the town grew until it reached its peak, probably in the mid-1930s. The mine worked good all the while up 'til the depression when it had to shut down for a while before starting up again.

"Of course, the Peabody mine is closed and there is no work here now. I never worked in the mines," he explains, then laughs at a suggestion he might be glad of it. "Oh, I don't know."

The post office remains as do two taverns. "All coal mining towns have taverns," he says, smiling again. "The last count I heard was that 600 and some people still live here."

Universal, it seems, survives mostly on its past.

* * *

We drive south from Universal past the Peabody mine that is quiet now, a sharp contrast to the days when heavy machines traversed the area. It is good to see that much of the area that was mined has been reclaimed, vegetation replacing the harshness of slag and naked earth.

VIGO COUNTY

Established in 1818, two years after Indiana became a state. Population 106,500. Named for Colonel Francis Vigo, who served with General George Rogers Clark. Terre Haute is the largest city and county seat. Industry and agriculture are both important.

In Vigo County, we drive northwest on U.S. 150 to Libertyville which is near the state line. Not much remains in Libertyville, a farm community built along the highway.

We return to Shirkieville, another small town with a tavern/restaurant, and drive south on Hollingsville Place Road. Vigo County roads, we soon note are named, rather than numbered. Mushroom hunters are out on the spring day.

The rich farm land stretches south of Shirkieville until the terrain gradually changes, from flat to rolling, from fields to wooded areas.

A resident, coffee cup in hand, inspects his newly-planted garden. He returns a wave, a smile on his face, another friendly Hoosier who knows no stranger.

We reach Yuma Road and drive southeast toward St. Mary-of-the-Woods, identified by the sign on the post office. The name "St. Mary" is common here, it is on the fire department, it is on the Catholic Church, it is St. Mary's Supper Club, which, unfortunately, won't open until 4 p.m. to serve "sirloin for two, spaghetti, veal, prime rib and a variety of seafood." It is an opportunity for Terre Haute residents to dine away from city traffic and the noise of the interstates.

A general store advertises, "This Ol' Store Now Open."

The village of St. Mary is the home of St. Mary-of-the-Woods, the nation's oldest Catholic liberal arts college for women. Its 1,200 students can choose from 29 majors. The college, operated by the Sisters of Providence, claims to be the first college in Indiana to offer an early childhood special education major. It is one of only 20 colleges in the country to offer a bachelor's degree in equestrian studies.

The campus is in the center of mature trees among Italian Renaissance-style buildings. The college, five miles across the Wabash River from Terre Haute is aggressively recruiting students, running TV ads and promoting "Discover The Woods." The College Marriott is open for Sunday brunches.

* * *

The area north of I-70 and between the Wabash River and the Illinois border is primarily a residential area of modest homes.

Except for West Terre Haute, a town of 2,500, there are no towns, just unincorporated communities like Marion Heights, Larimer Hill, Whitcomb Heights and older places such as Liggett and Ferguson Hill, which are difficult to find. The terrain is rolling to hilly, good for building sites.

Steve Sollara is riding a motorbike in a place he identifies as "Graceland," an area of 25 or so homes. He lives in the West Vigo

High School district but attends Terre Haute South which, he says, "has a better auto shop."

This is basically a blue collar community, which explains his interest in auto repair.

We follow his directions to Liggett. There are no signs, no stores, no churches to identify the community, only a resident who says, "This is it." It is a community without definition, one where the only business activity is a community yard sale.

* * *

We cross over I-70 and traverse a triangular area bounded on the east and south by the Wabash, the west by the Illinois border. A number of farms are in the area not heavily developed except for some suburban residences that are home to those who desire quiet surroundings where traffic is light and life is quiet.

New homes are in sharp contrast to a two-story farmstead with a bell tower just off Darwin Road. We drive to the PSI Energy power station on the banks of the Wabash. There are no bridges across the river and we return to I-70 and drive east to Terre Haute.

* * *

Ind. 63 turns southwest out of Terre Haute through the community of Prairieton, about four miles from the state line. A dozen or so homes are along the highway. So are a bakery, a post office, an abandoned auto repair shop and a general store that is now an upholstery shop.

A road west out of Prairieton leads near the location where the Wabash begins to form the western boundary of Indiana.

Near the river, in an area drained by the Greenfield Bayou, the blacktop changes to gravel, the houses become newer. A mail carrier, packages stacked on the dashboard of his pickup truck, already is out although the day is young. A lonesome silo, circled with trees, still stands, its barn and farm home gone.

A levee protects the farms from the Wabash as the road turns southeast through swamps. Trees and wasteland cover the land, except for some houses at river's edge.

It is here the river arcs west from the state line, taking Indiana into what otherwise would be Illinois.

HUTTON
Church Is Out

We find the town of Hutton, which would be on the state line if the artificial north-south boundary of the states had not been broken by the Wabash.

Not much is left in Hutton, a church in need of paint no longer is in use despite efforts to revive it. "No trespassing" and "Keep out" signs are tacked to its peeling weatherboarding, worshipers no longer welcome.

A few nice houses are amid some less attractive buildings and a junky area. A sign at one home warns, "Beware of Pit Bull." Horses graze inside an electric fence. A few oil wells are in the area.

West of Hutton, where flooding is frequent, houses are few and far between, almost lost in the expansive flat and fertile acreage that is bisected by gravel roads. Ahead the river banks are lined with trees. We have reached the end of the road.

* * *

We stop to talk to a woman who doesn't comprehend why anyone in his right mind would want to follow the river in this area.

She is more interested in the headlines in the *Terre Haute Star-Tribune* she has just taken from the box than in talking with a stranger in search of the state's geography.

She does concur that we have been in Hutton as we had suspected.

We return through Hutton, then attempt to search out the town of Vigo.

* * *

At a farm home southeast of Hutton, a man is at work with a welder. He removes his hood and greets us, warmly, not as reserved as the woman back nearer the river.

"Robert Axe," he says, without hesitation, adjusting the Gutwein Seeds cap on his head. He is wearing a denim jacket, the work uniform of a farmer. He puts down his welder and talks, easily, openly, interestingly.

Axe is using the welder, he says, to build a horse-drawn walking plow. Tractors are all right for others, but Axe likes horses.

He grew up in Terre Haute, where he helped care for a neighbor's horse, later had his own and developed a love for the animals he maintains even now that he is in his 60s.

No man is a stranger long with Axe. He shares his interests, talks about his life, about meeting his wife in Europe in the early 1950s when he was in the Army, about remaining in Germany for six months after his discharge.

He returned to America with his bride, moved to the small farm east of Hutton and worked at a Terre Haute steel fabricating plant until it moved south.

Now retired he farms about 20 acres with Belgium horses, breaking the ground with a riding plow he also made.

"I don't like tractors," he admits. "I don't like getting off and on to open gates," he explains as a smile crosses his face.

Axe recalls the days when the communities of Hutton and Vigo each had a store and a blacksmith shop. "My uncle, Ed Dent, once ran the store in Hutton," he says. "It burned in the early 1960s and was never replaced."

The Darwin Ferry that once operated on the Wabash at the southern edge of Vigo County is still in operation. It is now owned by farmers, he says, and no longer carries cars or passengers because of the high cost of insurance.

We leave Axe to his welder and plow. He knows his place in life and likes it. Everyone should be as fortunate.

* * *

We drive south through a rural area drained by Prairie Creek. We do not find Vigo, but we aren't too disappointed. People in the area don't know where it is either.

At the Pleasant Valley Church, a young mother, carrying an infant, doesn't hesitate to talk even though we are strangers. We ask her about Vigo, the community.

"You mean Vigo County?" she asks. "No, Vigo, the town," we reply. She has never heard of Vigo, the community, even though she can't be more than a couple of miles from where it is marked on the map.

"This is Prairie Creek," she explains. We decide Vigo is a ghost town that no longer exists.

West of Prairie Creek, two men salvage bricks from what once was a grade school, now fenced and privately owned.

SULLIVAN COUNTY

Established 1816 and named for Gen. Daniel Sullivan, a Revolutionary War hero. Population 19,000. County shares two recreation areas, Shakamak State Park and the Greene-Sullivan State Forest. Coal and agriculture are important to economy.

———

An unwelcome crop of mustard weeds paint a field yellow along the Vigo-Sullivan county line. Chuckholes as big as lakes make driving an adventure near the river.

The land is rolling and hilly, the few rural homes modest, the fields small, the roads lined with brush and trees.

We are not far from the site of the Fairbanks Massacre. A Lieutenant Fairbanks and his men were en route from Fort Knox with a supply wagon bound for besieged Fort Harrison near Terre Haute when ambushed by Indians. Fairbanks and seven of his soldiers were killed in the massacre on September 15, 1812. Only two of the men escaped to relate the incident.

* * *

We are in an area of the state that again juts out to the west as the river makes another of its many bends. The roads are now paved, the land somewhat rolling.

Suddenly the land becomes more fertile and the fields larger. Emission from the Merom power plant can be seen to the southeast for the horizon is unobstructed.

At Roads 800 West and 600 North, the terrain again changes. Brush lines the road which turns from blacktop to crushed stone. A nice rural home, quiet and serene, is off the road over a wooden bridge spanning a small stream.

Again the fields are smaller, the land more rolling with woods and trees instead of open fields. The pavement varies from blacktop to stone to blacktop.

* * *

We reach Ind. 154 which crosses the Wabash into the Illinois town of Hutsonville, population 700, at the western most point in Sullivan County. The highway slices through flat bottom land to the river bridge, the only span of the river from Terre Haute to Vincennes.

GRAYSVILLE
Sagamore Of The Wabash

We return on Ind. 154 to Graysville, a town that reflects the real Indiana. It is a place where folks care about each other, where there is no pretense.

It is a place where no visit is complete without a stop at Ralph's Marathon. Ralph is Ralph Ham, a man we have met on a previous visit. He remembers our name as he has that of hundreds of others who have stopped over the years.

Ralph is a Graysville fixture. He has operated the station, where he once serviced cars, since 1949. He also drove a school bus for 40 years before retiring at the end of the 1995 school year. It was a record, unmatched by few drivers, one that earned him a Sagamore of the Wabash award from Gov. Evan Bayh.

"I bought 10 new buses," he says, adding, "one every four years."

His gas station, snack shop, soda pop and story-telling-emporium probably is the most popular spot in town, at least for men. Women may prefer the post office, but that's okay. Their husbands probably feel freer to express themselves among a male-only crowd. A retired teacher, a farmer and his son and three other men are here today, all as friendly as Ralph. Each is eager to talk about the Graysville of yesterday as well as today.

Ham's station is not far from the school, once Graysville High, now an elementary.

The area around Graysville is Turman country. It is Turman Township. It is Turman Creek and the school officially was Turman Township High School. William Turman was a pioneer farmer in the area, working the land long before many areas of the state were settled.

Out west of town is the Mann-Turman Prairie Center where graves are located on a prehistoric Indian mound. The first Caucasians to be buried there were two of William Henry Harrison's men, who — while en route to the Battle of Tippecanoe — are said to have renewed a family feud and fought to their death.

Not far from the cemetery is the site of Fort Turman, which was used during the War of 1812. Land for the fort, which was a communication connection between Harrison's army in Ohio and at Vincennes, was donated by Turman.

MEROM
Time Stands Still

Merom, a river town rich in history, is four miles south of Graysville on Ind. 63. It was laid out in 1817 on the highest bluff above the Wabash River. Historians say it was named for a high lake along the Jordan River where, in Biblical times, Joshua fought a battle against kings.

It is at Merom where both Ind. 63 and Ind. 58 end. There is no bridge over the Wabash and chances are none could be built because of the elevation which contrasts to the lowland along the river on the Illinois side.

A historical marker notes the site of a log courthouse which served as Sullivan County's seat of government from 1819 to 1842.

Merom was an important river port as well as stop on a stage route along the Harrison Trail, the route Gen. Harrison's troops followed on their 1811 march to Tippecanoe.

A bell in the town park, presented by alumni, marks the site of the old Merom High School, again reflecting the pride Hoosiers have in the high schools they attended. Students from Merom now attend Sullivan High.

We again visit Merom Bluff — one of our favorite spots in Indiana — 150 to 170 feet over the river, high above the Illinois lowlands to the west. At Merom Bluff park, the ledge is lined with a stone wall.

The park is a place for visitors to pause and reflect on the days when Billy Sunday preached, Williams Jennings Bryan orated and

Carry Nation pleaded for temperance when they — along with thousands of others — came to take part in the chautauquas held each year from 1905-1936.

Merom still has an annual festival, the first weekend of June, that attracts up to 5,000 people a day for three days.

As we learned earlier in our visit for the book *Backroads Indiana*, time stands still here above the river. It is a good place to forget the time of day, or the day of the weekend, or the year of the calendar . . . at least for a while.

Across town from the park is the Merom Conference Center, once Union Christian College, which was a preparatory school and college from 1862 to 1924. It has been operated since 1936 by the United Church of Christ and is now a camp, conference center and recreational area.

Not many businesses remain in town, a general store being the only retail outlet. No matter. It is a town that survives on its past as well as its present.

Not far from town is the Merom Cemetery where some of Gen. Harrison's soldiers are buried. Part of the graveyard was the site of Fort Azatlan, which is said to have been erected by Middle Mississippian mound builders around 1200 A.D.

* * *

To the southeast is Merom Station, a town that grew up beside the railroad in 1854. A grain elevator next to the tracks no longer is in business and little else remains.

A welcome sign is outside the sandstone Merom Station Methodist Church but it does not appear to be the center of a thriving congregation. Merom Station is home to 20 families, but there is no post office, no businesses, just reminders of when the town was an important railroad stop.

* * *

The old community of Riverton was southwest of Merom Station near the river's edge. It, too, was a railroad town whose obituary was written with the decline of the railroad.

Today Riverton appears to be only a pumping station, no longer in use.

Good land, flat fields, and huge farm operations are in this area not far from the river. Some of the on-farm storage facilities are as big as grain elevators in small towns.

A crushed stone road winds near river's edge past a big sand and gravel business. A windmill rusts at an abandoned farmstead, the land taken over by a bigger operator with more resources.

Near Carlisle the fields again are large, the land flat, the corn, already four inches tall on May 11, irrigated with water that is plentiful near the river.

The town of Carlisle is in the distance to the southeast. To the west a levee protects the lowland from the Wabash. We again reach the river at Road 850 South and 500 West.

* * *

Some roads through parts of southwestern Sullivan County run almost at field level with no side ditches on either side. We continue south past watermelon and cantaloupe fields, the plants growing through a plastic cover which keeps out the weeds.

We jog west, south, east and west, staying as close to the river as possible. It is an isolated area with few houses, the only sounds being small stones pinging against the pickup on the unpaved road.

We have learned that to follow the river it is necessary to backtrack. A compass is a must . . . even though the bumps and potholes may knock it akilter at times. Some roads have 40 mph speed limits, but they are not needed. The roads are so rough no motorist would dare drive that fast, anyhow. Sections of roads in front of houses are coated with asphalt, perhaps a county commissioner's way of quelling complaints about roads which coat furniture in rural homes with dust.

* * *

Busseron Creek cuts through the area where irrigation equipment is common. A short distance away, the land changes to rolling and wooded, then abruptly the terrain levels out, the farms grow larger, the farms more fertile. The changes are dramatic, further evidence of Indiana's diversity.

* * *

We have reached Knox County, not far from Vincennes where we started this venture. Again we are in prime land where farms have huge metal storage granaries and well-maintained farm homes.

Here in the northwestern corner of the county is Shaker Prairie Christian Church and the Shepherd Cemetery, both dating back to 1820. We are northwest of Oaktown in a rural area that once was occupied by a community of Shakers, known officially as the United Society of Believers in Christ's Second Appearing.

The Shakers settled in the area in the early 1800s, according to historians, the term Shakers coming from their dance-like movements during services. They believed in a mother-father God, whose revelations — to be fully realized — required the appearance of a male and a female Christ, Jesus and Mother Ann Lee.

It is said Issachar Bates — along with others — ordered that celibacy be practiced, which was okay for him since he had already fathered 11 children. Deaths from malaria, caused by the swamps nearby, and a decline in conversions led to the abandonment of Shakertown in 1827.

The area near Busseron Creek is still known as Shaker Prairie.

We are in sand country, an area that allows Knox County to claim it is the watermelon capital of the state, a boast Jackson and a few other counties may dispute.

OAKTOWN

Farm Center

An elevated water tower draws us to Oaktown, a hamlet on the west side of U.S. 41 in the heart of watermelon, cantaloupe and peach farms.

It is obvious the business area is not as busy as it once was. Most store fronts are closed, but a gas station, bank and post office remain. So does the Long Branch saloon and Oaktown lounge. A farm co-op operation is at the south edge of town along the railroad.

* * *

We see more wheat than we have seen elsewhere in Indiana in the rolling fields south of Oaktown. Again, the terrain flattens and the fields become more expansive. Near the river, the open land changes to woods.

We pass moon-shaped Marie Pond, which is several acres in size, and hear the croaking of frogs. We recall the days of our youth when frogs were caught in other ponds and their legs skewered in a skillet over an open fire.

Chuckholes, big enough to bury a pickup, make driving difficult. It is difficult to maintain smooth roads in areas subject to flooding.

EMISON

East of the river is the town of Emison, marked by a sign, "Established in 1867. Population 87." It was a bigger place back in the days when the nation moved on rails and trains stopped on their route between Vincennes and Oaktown.

A grain elevator along the railroad is now abandoned. The two-story home of the Oddfellows Lodge is closed. A Pioneer Seed Company dealership appears to be the only business in town.

Open for play is a park operated by the Emison United Methodist Church for the Emison Youth Foundation. The church appears to be the hub of social as well as religious life of the community.

A few junk cars, seemingly a requirement for many small towns, remain in one or two yards. A pile of used tires is another eyesore.

* * *

It is lunch, time to stop at Dyball's Restaurant on U.S. 41 between Emison and Oaktown. A server recommends the giant homemade breaded tenderloin, $3.50. It is a wise choice, a sandwich large enough for a full meal.

We have learned on this trip around Indiana that most Hoosiers, regardless of the area of the state, know good food when they serve it.

A STATE OF CONTRASTS

We continue on to Vincennes, our trek around the border of Indiana at an end. The journey has increased our appreciation of the diversity of the state, given us new insight about its people, taught us that there is no simple definition for "Hoosier."

He may be a steelworker in a metroplex domed by smog, he may be a farmer in a limitless horizon, he may operate locks on the Ohio River, or load freight on an ocean liner at Burns Harbor. She may be a postmaster in Pleasant Mills. a game warden or a businesswoman in a Fortune 500 company in Evansville.

Home may be a shack on the Ohio or a castle on Lake Michigan. A favorite restaurant may be at Leavenworth Overlook, on Lake Michigan, or a coffee shop in farm country.

The soil may be sand, clay, loam or muck. The topography may be board flat or craggily rugged; fields small fenced patches between hills or up to 640 acres and limited only by county roads.

It may be only an impression, but residents in the north appear to be more reserved, less open, less likely to volunteer information than those along the Ohio River.

Life is slower in the south, traffic is lighter, the daily grind less wearing. The scenery is more diverse in the south, the secrets more numerous, perhaps because the roads are more winding, less traveled, and fewer visitors have discovered the treasures that are there.

Yet each area of the state has its own surprises. They await the curious, who will not be disappointed if they choose to seek them out.

ALSO BY WENDELL TROGDON

NOSTALGIA

Those Were The Days
Through the Seasons
Carved in Memory
Back Home
The Country Bumpkin Gang

TRAVEL

Backroads Indiana

BIOGRAPHY

Out Front: The Cladie Bailey Story

BASKETBALL

No Harm No Foul: Referees are People, Too
Gym Rats: Sons Who Play For Fathers Who Coach
Shooting Stars: Trek to the Championship
Basket Cases: High School Basketball Coaches
Whistle Blowers: A No Harm No Foul Sequel

The author was a co-author with Damon Bailey
of the book, *Damon — Living A Dream.*

For more information about these books write:
Wendell Trogdon
P.O. Box 651
Mooresville IN, 46158